Quod scriptura, non iubet vetat

The Latin translates, "What is not commanded in scripture, is forbidden:'

On the Cover: Baptists rejoice to hold in common with other evangelicals the main principles of the orthodox Christian faith. However, there are points of difference and these differences are significant. In fact, because these differences arise out of God's revealed will, they are of vital importance. Hence, the barriers of separation between Baptists and others can hardly be considered a trifling matter. To suppose that Baptists are kept apart solely by their views on Baptism or the Lord's Supper is a regrettable misunderstanding. Baptists hold views which distinguish them from Catholics, Congregationalists, Episcopalians, Lutherans, Methodists, Pentecostals, and Presbyterians, and the differences are so great as not only to justify, but to demand, the separate denominational existence of Baptists. Some people think Baptists ought not teach and emphasize their differences but as E.J. Forrester stated in 1893, "Any denomination that has views which justify its separate existence, is bound to promulgate those views. If those views are of sufficient importance to justify a separate existence, they are important enough to create a duty for their promulgation ... the very same reasons which justify the separate existence of any denomination make it the duty of that denomination to teach the distinctive doctrines upon which its separate existence rests." If Baptists have a right to a separate denominational life, it is their duty to propagate their distinctive principles, without which their separate life cannot be justified or maintained.

Many among today's professing Baptists have an agenda to revise the Baptist distinctives and redefine what it means to be a Baptist. Others don't understand why it even matters. The books being reproduced in the *Baptist Distinctives Series* are republished in order that Baptists from the past may state, explain and defend the primary Baptist distinctives as they understood them. It is hoped that this Series will provide a more thorough historical perspective on what it means to be distinctively Baptist.

The Lord Jesus Christ asked, *"And why call ye me, Lord, Lord, and do not the things which I say?"* (Luke 6:46). The immediate context surrounding this question explains what it means to be a true disciple of Christ. Addressing the same issue, Christ's question is meant to show that a confession of discipleship to the Lord Jesus Christ is inconsistent and untrue if it is not accompanied with a corresponding submission to His authoritative commands. Christ's question teaches us that a true recognition of His authority as Lord inevitably includes a submission to the authority of His Word. Hence, with this question Christ has made it forever impossible to separate His authority as King from the authority of His Word. These two principles—the authority of Christ as King and the authority of His Word—are the two most fundamental Baptist distinctives. The first gives rise to the second and out of these two all the other Baptist distinctives emanate. As F.M. Iams wrote in 1894, "Loyalty to Christ as King, manifesting itself in a constant and unswerving obedience to His will as revealed in His written Word, is the real source of all the Baptist distinctives:' In the search for the *primary* Baptist distinctive many have settled on the Lordship of Christ as the most basic distinctive. Strangely, in doing this, some have attempted to separate Christ's Lordship from the authority of Scripture, as if you could embrace Christ's authority without submitting to what He commanded. However, while Christ's Lordship and Kingly authority can be isolated and considered essentially for discussion's sake, we see from Christ's own words in Luke 6:46 that His Lordship is really inseparable from His Word and, with regard to real Christian discipleship, there can be no practical submission to the one without a practical submission to the other.

In the symbol above the Kingly Crown and the Open Bible represent the inseparable truths of Christ's Kingly and Biblical authority. The Crown and Bible graphics are supplemented by three Bible verses (Ecclesiastes 8:4, Matthew 28:18-20, and Luke 6:46) that reiterate and reinforce the inextricable connection between the authority of Christ as King and the authority of His Word. The truths symbolized by these components are further emphasized by the Latin quotation - *quod scriptura, non iubet vetat*— i.e., "What is not commanded in scripture, is forbidden:' This Latin quote has been considered historically as a summary statement of the regulative principle of Scripture. Together these various symbolic components converge to exhibit the two most foundational Baptist Distinctives out of which all the other Baptist Distinctives arise. Consequently, we have chosen this composite symbol as a logo to represent the primary truths set forth in the *Baptist Distinctives Series*.

The Tri-Lemma;

OR,

DEATH BY THREE HORNS.

J. R. Graves
1820-1893

The Tri-Lemma;

OR,

DEATH BY THREE HORNS.

THE PRESBYTERIAN GENERAL ASSEMBLY NOT ABLE
TO DECIDE THIS QUESTION:

"IS BAPTISM IN THE ROMISH CHURCH VALID?"

AFFIRMATIVELY OR NEGATIVELY WITHOUT UNBAPTIZING
AND UNCHURCHING THE WHOLE PROTESTANT WORLD!

NO PROTESTANT CAN DECIDE IT, AND SAVE HIS
BIBLE AND HIS BAPTISM.

BY

J. R. GRAVES, LL.D.,

AUTHOR OF "GREAT IRON WHEEL," ETC., ETC., EDITOR OF
THE TENNESSEE BAPTIST, NASHVILLE, TENN.

With a Biographical Sketch of the Author by John Franklin Jones

NASHVILLE:
SOUTH-WESTERN PUBLISHING HOUSE.
1861

he Baptist Standard Bearer, Inc.
NUMBER ONE IRON OAKS DRIVE • PARIS, ARKANSAS 72855

Thou hast given a *standard* to them that fear thee;
that it may be displayed because of the truth.
— Psalm 60:4

Reprinted 2006

by

THE BAPTIST STANDARD BEARER, INC.
No. 1 Iron Oaks Drive
Paris, Arkansas 72855
(479) 963-3831

THE WALDENSIAN EMBLEM
lux lucet in tenebris
"The Light Shineth in the Darkness"

ISBN# 1579785123

PREFACE.

THE discussions, admissions, and conclusion of the N. S. Presbyterian General Assembly, were by that body evidently desired and attempted to be kept from the Presbyterian membership and the masses of the American people.

The desire and design of the author, or rather compiler of this little work, is to place the admissions and confessions made in that body in the hands of every American Christian and citizen—they belong to them. Will the reader aid in its general circulation?

"Go through, go through the gates; prepare ye the way of the people; cast up, cast up the highway; gather out the stones; lift up a standard for the people."

INTRODUCTION.

TRI-LEMMA! Tri-lemma! It is not in the Dictionaries. Pray, what is a tri-lemma? asks the Reader.

When one is pinned between two difficulties, we say he is in a Di-lemma.

When he is pinned between two difficulties, and pierced through by a third, may we not say he is in a

TRI-LEMMA?

Read and decide if Protestantism is not in just such a situation.

J. R. G.

NASHVILLE, Jan. 1, 1860.

CONTENTS.

CHAPTER I.

THE QUESTION DISCUSSED.

Its importance to all Protestant sects—The difficulties it presents—The attention given to it by the O. S. and N. S. Presbyterian Assemblies,... 9

CHAPTER II.

THE POSITION OF THE O. S. PRESBYTERIAN ASSEMBLY.

Its answer fatal to the Ecclesiastical claims of Presbyterians and all Protestants,.. 15

CHAPTER III.

POSITION OF THE N. S. PRESBYTERIAN ASSEMBLY, 1854.

The question submitted to a Committee—A Majority and Minority Report—The Assembly divided—It is found that to decide Romish baptisms valid or invalid was equally fatal to the baptisms of all Protestants—Decided that it could not expediently be decided—The Trilemma,... 52

CHAPTER IV.

TWO OTHER QUESTIONS.

PAGE

1. Can Protestants oppose the Papacy without being slain by the Papacy?—2. Can Baptists oppose the Papacy without destroying Protestantism?.......................... 80

CHAPTER V.

THE ECCLESIASTICAL CLAIMS OF BAPTISTS.

Did Baptists originate in the bosom of the Papal Church, or receive their baptisms and ordinations from the Man of Sin?... 119

The Tri-lemma;

OR,

DEATH BY THREE HORNS.

CHAPTER I.

THE QUESTION UNDER CONSIDERATION.

Its Importance to all Protestant Sects—The Difficulties it presents—The Attention given it by the Old School and New School Presbyterian Assemblies.

THE question that has presented itself to Protestants as embarrassed with more difficulties than any other, and the solution of which they have discovered must prove fatal to their ecclesiastical claims in the eyes of the world, whether answered affirmatively or negatively, is this:

Is Baptism in the Church of Rome Valid?

From what has appeared, it is evident that there is a growing uneasiness felt by the more intelligent and thinking Pedobaptist ministers, generally, and by Presbyterians, ministers and members, especially.

That Presbyterians, more than the other Protestant societies, are more disturbed by this question, is owing to the fact that it has been up and discussed at length in the General Assemblies of both the Old and New School divisions of the Presbyterian family. The positions taken by their leading doctors of divinity, and the utterances they gave during the discussions that arose, so far as they have been heard, have startled and alarmed their people! So convinced were the leaders that a knowledge of the discussions, and of the difficulties surrounding the question, by their people, would be productive of great disquiet, if not of more serious consequences, that they have, as much as possible, kept them in ignorance, and discouraged discussion in their denominational papers.

But this is one of those questions that can not be suffocated. Inquiry once started can not be stifled down. If the people are allowed to hear but little, and not allowed to talk or to write about it, yet they can *think;* and they will *think* more and more about it. Thus will investigation go forward, producing conviction, until the masses are permeated, and when they do act— when they do call their leaders to an account— it will be a fearful reckoning. The volcanic fires, though long restrained by the superincumbent pressure, yet burn silently, constantly gathering strength and force, until they burst through their rocky barriers to the surface, and pour their irresistible fiery currents of destruction over the land.

The time, we think, has fully come when not only *Christian Protestants* should meet this question fairly and fully, but *all men* should understand its bearings. Men of no ecclesiastical connections are called upon to support, and they all are supporting, some one of the religious denominations by their means and influence, and they have a right to understand the question.

It is the spirit of the Papacy, whose power is the power of darkness, to repress free thought, and the liberty of speech and the press. It is a confession of a consciousness of wrong, on the part of the leaders of the people or the officers of any government, civil or ecclesiastical, to seek protection by pursuing such a course.

The writer's design in this little work is to submit to the reading world all the facts, admissions and conclusions, etc., etc., connected with the discussion of this question by the Presbyterian General Assemblies, that its grave importance, and the fatal difficulties with which it is invested to all *Protestants*,* may be clearly understood, and that candid men may act in accordance with their convictions from the facts.

There are several axioms that should be borne in mind by the reader throughout this discussion. They are held in common by all parties.

1. THAT NO ORGANIZATION BUT A TRUE CHURCH OF CHRIST, VISIBLE, CAN ADMINISTER SCRIPTURAL BAPTISM.

2. CONVERSELY, IF THE BAPTISM IS CONSIDERED SCRIPTURAL AND

---

* Baptists are not Protestants. "They are the only people that never symbolized with the Papacy."—*Sir I. Newton.* (See Tract. Price 10 Cents.)

VALID, THE SOCIETY ADMINISTERING IT MUST BE ACKNOWLEDGED AND TREATED AS A TRUE CHURCH OF CHRIST, VISIBLE.

Now, all can see if the baptisms of the Church of Rome are pronounced Scriptural and valid, then the Church of Rome must be admitted to be a *true church* of Christ, visible.

But if Protestants admit this, they surrender their own claims to be true churches of Christ, because they, in separating from the true Church of Christ, become schismatics. But they were excluded and anathematized by the true Church, and therefore their ministers were deprived of all authority to baptize, or to administer Church ordinances.

But should Protestants deny the validity of Romish baptisms, they would thereby deny that the Church of Rome is a Scriptural church, and consequently that she could administer valid ordinances.

By taking this ground, all can again see that they would effectually destroy themselves—for no Christian Pedobaptist has any other baptism than he received from the priests of Rome. Luther, Calvin, Zwingle, Knox, and all the first ministers, and all those who composed the first societies of the Reformers, were baptized by Roman Catholic priests, and in the Church of Rome, and consequently their baptisms are unscriptural and invalid. But if their baptisms are invalid, then their societies can not be considered churches in any sense, as there can be no church without baptism; and if not churches, Protestant ministers have no Scriptural right either to preach the Gospel, or baptize others into their societies! Moreover, by so doing they deceive and mislead the people, causing them to believe they are baptized, when, in fact, they are not; causing the people to believe that they are in visible churches of Christ, when, in fact, and according to the admissions of these leaders, they are not, but in human societies, that can never administer the ordinances of Christ's Church!!

That the above are plain statements of facts, the following history will show.

CHAPTER II.

THE QUESTION AMONG PRESBYTERIANS.

The Report of the Old School General Assembly in 1845—Its Answer fatal to the Ecclesiastical Claims of Presbyterians and all Protestants.

THE question of the validity of Romish baptisms has been up for discussion no less than three times before the Presbyterian General Assembly, within the past few years; and with each discussion and attempt to settle it, the more unsettled it appears to be left, and the greater the dissatisfaction arising from it. We have not at hand a digest of the acts of the Assembly, but from the Report below, we find that this question has vexed Presbyterian Assemblies since the year 1790, and has been bequeathed, unsettled, to each succeeding generation.

It was before Parliament so early as 1558, as we shall see.

So early as 1790, Presbyterians decided that the Romish Church was not a true church, and her ordinances, therefore, invalid.

It appeared in 1829, and was indefinitely postponed, for reasons given by one who was at that time a member of the Assembly:

"I was in the General Assembly of the Presbyterian Church in 1829, (a body of about two hundred members,) when a question was sent us for decision: 'Are the baptisms of Popish priests to be accepted by our [Presbyterian] Churches as valid baptisms?' It was discussed, and we should have voted 'No,' nearly unanimously; but an influential and more shrewd one —secretly reflecting that *all* our baptisms originally came from Popery—moved and obtained an indefinite postponement of the subject."*

It reappeared again in the year 1835, when the Assembly decided that the Romish Church was "apostate from Christ, and no true church," and her priests as usurpers of the sacred functions of the ministry, consequently, their baptisms null and void.

---

* J. F. Bliss, in "Popery and Protestantism Compared.'

But notwithstanding this strong decision, in 1845, the Presbytery of Ohio sent up the question for a *re*-settlement.

The General Assembly met in Cincinnati, O., May 15, 1835, and the following is its report, *in extenso*, on the subject:

REPORT.

"The committee appointed to draw up a minute expressive of the views of the Assembly, presented a Report which was read and adopted, and is as follows, viz.:

"The question presented to this Assembly by overture from the Presbytery of Ohio, '*Is baptism in the Church of Rome valid?*' is one of a very grave character, and of deep practical importance. The answer to it must involve principles vital to the peace, the purity, and the stability of the Church of God.

"After a full discussion, carried through several days, this Assembly has decided, by a nearly unanimous vote, that *baptism so administered is not valid;* because, since baptism is an ordinance established by Christ *in his Church*, (Form of Gov., ch. viii; Matt. xxviii: 19, 20,) and is to be administered *only by a minister of Christ*, duly called and ordained to be a steward of the mysteries of God, (Directory, ch. vii: sec. 1,) it follows that no rite administered by one *who is not himself a duly ordained minister* of the true Church of God, visible, can be regarded as an ordinance of Christ, whatever be the name by which it is called, whatever be the form employed in its administration. The so-called priests of the Romish communion are not ministers of Christ, for they are commissioned as agents of the Papal hierarchy, which is not a church of Christ, but the Man of Sin, apostate from the truth, the enemy of righteousness and of God. She has long [always] lain under the curse of God, who has called his people to come out of her, that they be not partakers of her plagues.

"It is the unanimous opinion of all the Reformed Churches, that the whole Papal body, though once a branch of the visible Church, has long since become utterly corrupt and hopelessly apostate. It was a conviction of this which led to the Reformation, and the complete separation of the Reformed body from the Papal communion. Luther and his coadjutors, being duly ordained presbyters at the time when they left the Romish communion, which then, though fearfully corrupt, was the only visible Church in the countries of their abode, were fully authorized by the Word of God to ordain successors in the ministry, and so to extend and perpetuate the Reformed Churches as true churches of Christ; while the contumacious adherence of Rome to her corruptions, as shown in the decisions of the Council of Trent, (which she adopts as authoritative,) cuts her off from the visible Church of Christ, as heretical and unsound. This was the opinion of the Reformers; and it is the doctrine of the Reformed Church to this day. In entire accordance with this is the decision of the General Assembly of our Church, passed in 1835, (see Minutes of General Assembly, vol. viii: page 33,) declaring the Church of Rome to be an apostate body.

"The decision by the General Assembly of 1835, renders the return of a negative to the inquiry proposed by the Presbytery of Ohio *indispensable on the ground of consistency;* unless we are prepared to admit, in direct contradiction to the standards of the Presbyterian Church, that baptism is not an ordinance established by Christ in his Church exclusively, and that it may be administered by an agent of the Man of Sin, an emissary of the Prince of darkness—that it may be administered in sport or in blasphemy, and yet be valid as though administered by a duly commissioned steward of the mysteries of God.

"Nor can it be urged that the Papal hierarchy is improving in her character, and gradually approximating to the Scriptural standard. She *claims to be infallible;* her dogmas she promulgates as the doctrine of heaven; and she pronounces her heaviest anathemas against any and every man who questions her authority, and refuses to bow to her doctrines. She can not recede from the ground she has assumed. She has adopted as her own the decisions of the Council of Trent, which degrade the Word of God, which claim equal authority for the Apocrypha as for the New Testament, and which declare the sense held and taught by the holy Mother Church, on the authority of tradition and of the fathers, to be the true and only sense of Scripture. All who deny this position, or who question her authority, she denounces with the bitterest curses.

"She thus perverts the truth of God, she rejects the doctrine of justification by faith, she substitutes human merit for the righteousness of Christ, and self-inflicted punishment for Gospel repentance; she proclaims her so-called baptism to be regeneration, and the reception of the consecrated wafer, in the Eucharist, to be the receiving of Christ himself, the source and fountain of grace, and with him all the grace he can impart. Is this the truth? Is reliance on this system true religion? Can, then, the Papal body be a church?

"The Church, (*i. e.*, the Church visible,) as defined in our standards, is the whole body of those persons, together with their children, who make professions of *the holy religion of Christ*, and of submission to his laws. (Form of Gov., ch. ii: sec. 2.) As certainly then, as the dogmas and practices of Papal Rome are not the *holy religion of Christ*, must it be considered that the Papal body is not a church of Christ at all; and if not, then her agents, be they styled priests, bishops, archbishops, cardinals, or pope, are not ministers of Christ in any sense, for they have no connection with his true, visible Church; and, not being true ministers of Christ, they have no power to administer Christian ordinances, and the rite they *call* baptism is not, in any sense, to be regarded as valid Christian baptism.

"Further, by the perverted meaning they affix, and the superstitious rites they have superadded to the ceremonies they perform under the name of baptism and the Eucharist, the symbolic nature and true design of both the ordinances of baptism and the Lord's Supper are lost sight of, and utterly destroyed; so that, could we by any possibility assign to her the *name of a church*, she would still be a church without the two grand ordinances of the Gospel; she neither administers Christian baptism nor celebrates the Supper of the Lord. Moreover, since, by the eleventh canon of the Council of Trent, she declares the efficacy of her ordinances to depend upon the *intention* of the administrator, no man can know with certainty that her form of administration, in any ordinance, is not a mere mockery; no consistent Papist can be certain that he has been duly baptized, or that he has received the veritable Eucharist; he can not *know* that the priest who officiates at his altar is a true priest, nor that there is actually any one true priest, nor any one prelate rightly consecrated in the whole Papal communion. The Papal hierarchy has, by her own solemn acts, shrouded all her doings in uncertainty, and enveloped all her rites in hopeless obscurity. Even on this ground alone, the validity of her baptism might safely be denied.

"Nor is the fact that instances now and then occur of apparent piety in the members of her communion, and of intelligence, zeal, and conscientiousness in some of her priests, any ground of objection against the position here taken by this Assembly. The virtues of individuals do not purify the body of which they are members. We are to judge of the character of a body claiming to be a church of Christ, not by the opinions or practices of individual members, but by its standards, and its allowed practices. Bound as he is by the authority of his Church, and that on pain of her heaviest malediction, to understand the Scriptures only in the sense in which his Church understands and explains them, a consistent Papist can not receive or hold the true religion, or the doctrines of grace. If he does, he must either renounce the Papacy, or, hypocritically, conceal his true sentiments, or he must prepare to brave the thunders of her wrath. True religion and an intelligent adherence to Papal Rome are utterly incompatible and impossible. The Church and the Papacy are the repelling poles of the moral system.

"Difficulties may possibly arise in individual cases. It may not be easy at all times to say whether an applicant for admission to the Church of Christ has, or has not, been baptized; whether he has been christened by a Popish priest or not. In all such doubtful cases, the session of a church must act according to the light before them. But it is safer, and more conducive to peace and edification, to embrace a well-established principle for our guidance, and act upon it firmly, in the fear of God, leaving all consequences with him, than to suffer ourselves, without any fixed principles, to lie at the mercy of circumstances.

"While some other Churches may hesitate to carry out fully the principles of the Reformation, in wholly repudiating Popish baptism, as well as the Popish mass, we, as Presbyterians, feel bound to act on the principle laid down by our Assembly so long ago as 1790, (see Digest, pp. 94, 95,) that, so long as a body is by us recognized as a true church, her ordinances are to be deemed valid, and no longer.

"In 1835, the Assembly declared the Papacy to be apostate from Christ, and no true church. As we do not recognize her as a portion of the visible Church of Christ, we can not consistently, view her priesthood as other than usurpers of the sacred functions of the ministry, her ordinances as unscriptural, and her baptism as totally invalid."

The religious world must entertain a profound respect for the matured decisions of such a body as the General Assembly of the Presbyterian

Church of America; and the Assembly of 1845 was said to have presented a "brilliant array of ministers in the first rank of intellectual endowment." The above Report, it must be conceded by all, is a masterly production. Its premises are unambiguous and eminently Scriptural. No Protestant or Baptist will gainsay them. The conclusion is invincible, that the Romish Church never had authority to administer baptism, or to ordain ministers who could administer valid baptism, because she was never a true church of Christ visible, but always apostate from the truth, and the "Man of Sin."

But has not the General Assembly as clearly demonstrated that Presbyterian and *all Protestant baptisms are no baptisms*, as it has that "there is no baptism in the Romish Church?"

We ask the serious, candid reader to compare the premises in the above Report, and the plain facts of history.

I. *If it be true that no baptism is valid unless administered by " a duly ordained minister of the true Church of God visible,"* (though we *should grant that the Church of Rome is, and ever has been, such a church,) even then no Presbyterian or Pedobaptist can have a reasonable assurance that he has been truly baptized.*

That Presbyterians, in common with all the Reformed or Protestant sects, received their baptisms and ordinations from the Romish apostasy, is denied by no one, is admitted by the Assembly itself.

That the Romish Church did, from its "first coming and working after the manner of Satan," corrupt the design and administration of baptism, is well known to the merest tyro in historical reading. She, at a very early day, before her universal Bishop sat upon the seven hills of Rome, in the seat, to exercise all the powers of the Dragon — Pagan Rome — ascribed a saving efficacy to baptism, and taught that without it there was no salvation. This led her to provide for its administration to all in every period of life, and under every necessitous circumstance. Under ordinary circumstances, the duly ordained priest was the appointed administrator; but, if in danger of death, and no priest was at hand, a layman; and if he could not be had, any one, male or female, a midwife, cook, or scullion, or even heretic, infidel, or Turk! and if water could not be procured, that wine, or milk, or *any fluid* might be used!!

Such was the sacredness of baptism in the eye of "Holy Mother," that when it was administered by boys in sport upon each other, it was held by her as valid baptism and conferring salvation!

It is related by Ruffinus, and indorsed by other writers, that Alexander, bishop of Alexandria, once saw a parcel of boys engaged in a play, called "boy bishop," in which they were wont to imitate all things usually performed in the Church, especially the administration of baptism. This worthy bishop conferred with a council of his clergy, and the conclave solemnly resolved, that "the baptism so administered by these boys in play was lawful and valid, and was not to be repeated."

Now, unquestionably, thousands and tens of thousands, received baptism in the Romish

Church by these informal and blasphemous ways, and it has been strongly said :*

"Who can tell, then, but that the Presbyterian Churches of America and Europe derived their baptism from a layman, a midwife, a cook, a scullion, an infidel, or a Turk?—or perhaps from some baptism administered by boys in sport? We fearlessly assert that no one can tell. And perhaps, too, their baptism was derived from a case where no water could be procured, and wine, or milk, or something of the sort, was used. And certainly, if *regularly* derived, it was administered in *greasy* water, for 'Holy Mother' requires oil to be poured in the water! At all events, is not the presumption irresistible in favor of their receiving it from those abandoned profligates who disgraced the priestly name during the dark ages; when, according to Chillingworth, 'of a hundred seeming priests, it was doubtful if there was one true one?'

"But who among the Papal officials may be considered a '*duly ordained minister* of the true church of God, visible?' Will our Presbyterian brethren claim to derive their baptism from his Holiness, the head of the Romish Church? No;

---

* Western Baptist Review, Vol. I, p. 12.

they esteem him no minister of Christ. Will they derive it from archbishops, bishops, priests, etc.? No; they affirm that no such officers belong to the 'true Church of God, visible.' Luther was ordained a *priest*, (not a *presbyter*, as the Assembly declares,) and the thought of it in after life made him shudder. The officiating bishop gave him the cup, and said, ' Receive the power of offering sacrifice for the living and the dead.' ' That the earth did not then swallow us both up,' says Luther, ' was an instance of the patience and long-suffering of the Lord!' He was a *priest*, and not a duly ordained minister of the true Church! And Calvin, if we may believe Beza, was never ordained even a priest. He never received ' orders in any other way than by *tonsure*.'* In a word, should their

---

* " The tonsure in the Romish Church may be received after the age of seven years. It is the first part of the ceremony of ordination. The candidate presents himself, in a black cassock, before the bishop, with a surplice on the right arm, and a lighted taper in his hand. He kneels, and the bishop standing, covered with his miter, repeats a prayer, and several verses from the Scriptures. The bishop, then sitting, cuts five different parcels of hair from the head of the candidate, who repeats these words, ' *The Lord is my inheritance.*' Putting off his miter, the bishop says a prayer over the person tonsured; an anthem is sung by the choir; then a prayer, in the middle of which

chain of succession not have been rudely broken by some layman, woman, 'boy bishop,' or infidel, still consistency compels the Presbyterians to recognize the Papal hierarchy as duly ordained ministers in the true Church—to admit, to say the least, that, in the Church of the Gospel dispensation, there is an established priesthood, not 'called of God, as was Aaron,' to offer gifts and sacrifices. All this, we say, must be admitted, and yet no Presbyterian will admit it; or else, according to the General Assembly, there is no baptism in the Presbyterian Church!"

But bad as this is, it is not the worst.

II. *In asserting that Calvin and Luther, and all the first ministers of the Reformation, received valid baptism in the Romish Church, as it does, the General Assembly annulled the baptisms of all Presbyterians and Pedobaptists!*

I submit the reasoning of the editor of the "Western Baptist Review" upon this proposition:

---

the bishop puts the surplice on the candidate for orders, and says, '*May the Lord clothe thee with thy new name.*' The ceremony is concluded by the candidate's presenting the wax taper to the bishop, who gives him his blessing."
—*Dr. Hurde's Rites and Ceremonies,* p. 282.

"If the Reformers were baptized at all, if their baptism was valid, (and this was taken for granted by the Assembly,) then they were baptized by those who were duly ordained ministers of 'the *true Church* of God, visible.' But they were baptized by priests of the Church of Rome; therefore, the Church of Rome was 'the true Church of God, visible,' at the time of the Reformation! Indeed, the General Assembly seems to have embraced fully this conclusion. It says: 'Luther and his coadjutors, being duly ordained presbyters [*alias* "priests"] at the time they left the Romish communion—which then, though fearfully corrupt, was the only visible Church in the countries of their abode— were fully authorized by the Word of God to ordain successors in the ministry, and so to extend the Reformed Churches, as true Churches of Christ.' Ay, it was necessary to the argument, not merely to affirm that the Romish was 'the only visible Church' in the countries of the Reformers, but that she was emphatically 'the true Church of God, visible;' or, according to the showing of the Assembly, Luther and his coadjutors could not administer the ordinances, and could not 'extend the Reformed Churches, as true Churches of Christ.' For, remember, the position is roundly maintained, that no one can administer the ordinances, unless ' duly ordained in the true Church of God, visible.' If Luther and his coadjutors were authorized to administer baptism—and the Assembly say they were—then, according to the same authority, they were duly ordained ministers of 'the true Church of God, visible; and we learn, from the same source, that they were ordained by the Romish Church!!!—thus making the Romish 'the true Church of God, visible'!!

"We do not question for a moment the right of the General Assembly to declare the Romish Church 'the true Church of God, visible,' in the days of the Reformers; but surely such a declaration, if received, must utterly destroy all confidence in the judgment of Luther and his coadjutors, who vehemently testified that the Church of Rome was Antichrist and the Whore of Babylon! But grant the assumption that Luther and his coadjutors were duly ordained presbyters in the Romish Church, or 'the true Church of God, visible,' and what follows? Why, that in leaving the Church in which they were 'duly ordained presbyters,' Luther and his coadjutors left 'the Church of God, visible!' This is so plain that the blind may see it. But this is not all—it is but the beginning For, if this Church could 'duly ordain' them, she could duly *depose* them. If she could give the power she could take it away. How, then, could Luther and his coadjutors be 'fully authorized by the Word of God to ordain successors in the ministry,' seeing that the Church that made them ministers—ay, 'the true Church of God, visible'—had deposed them from office, and solemnly excluded them from fellowship? Dr. Rice, in one of his speeches on this question, told the Assembly: 'If the Pope has the authority to put any one into the Church, he has authority to put out, and then we are all out, and we may as well quit the discussion, and go home.' Very true. The remark was worthy of the logical acumen of Dr. Rice. And it is just as true, that if the Romish Church had authority to baptize and 'duly ordain Luther and his coadjutors, she had the authority to depose them from office, and to exclude them. Indeed, the authority is the same, and can not be separated so as to extend to the one and not to the other. It does not matter whence the authority was derived—from heaven, earth, or hell—it was just the same in the one case as the other—was just as effectual in unmaking as in making them ministers, and in excluding them from, as including them in, the pale of 'the true Church of God, visible.' These conclusions are natural, necessary, and irresistible. If the Romish Church was the true Church, then the Reformers were deposed and excommunicated; if she was not the true Church, then they were never baptized, nor ordained to the ministry. Let the Presbyterians take either horn of this dilemma, and, their General Assembly being witness, they are without baptism, without a ministry, and without a Church!"

Once more:

III. *The Papal hierarchy, at the time of the Reformation, was no more the true Church of Christ, visible, than now, and her baptisms, therefore, were no more valid then than they are to-day.*

The same editor says:

"Examine all the arguments advanced by the General Assembly to prove that the Romish Church is no Church, and her baptism no baptism, and do they not apply with equal force and power to her condition at the time of, and prior to, the Reformation? 'The so-called priests of the Romish communion,' says the Assembly, 'are not ministers of Christ, for they are commissioned as agents of the Papal hierarchy, which is not a Church of Christ, but the Man of Sin, apostate from the truth, the enemy of righteousness and of God.' And what were Luther and his coadjutors, when priests in the Romish communion, but the commissioned agents of the Papal hierarchy, and the *sworn vassals* of the Pope of Rome? It was not the Reformation, nor yet the decision of the Presbyterian General Assembly, in 1835, 'declaring the Church of Rome an apostate body, that made it so. That society, controlled by and subservient to, the Papal hierarchy, *never was* 'the true Church of God, visible.' The Church in Rome, founded by the apostles, and the Papal hierarchy, were never identified, never had any relationship, and were always as opposite to each other as light and darkness. The coming of the Papacy was 'after the working of Satan, [*not* of the apostles,] with all power, and signs, and lying wonders, and with all deceivableness of unrighteousness, in them that perish.' From the beginning, it was 'the Man of Sin and Son of Perdition, who opposeth and exalteth himself above all that is called God, or that is worshiped; so that he, as God, sitteth in the temple of God, showing himself that he is God.' (2 Thess. ii : 4, 9, and 10.) The Papacy, according to Protestants, 'ascended out of the bottomless pit, and shall go into perdition,' and has been, from the first, full of the names of blasphemy—'Mystery, Babylon the great, the mother of harlots, and abominations of the earth.' (Rev. xvii, *passim*.) Protestant commentators tell us that Daniel the prophet foretold the rise and reign of the Papal Church in the 'little horn' that came up among the ten horns of the fourth beast, 'before whom there were three of the first horns plucked up by the roots; and, behold, in this horn were eyes like the eyes of a man, and a mouth speaking great things.' 'And the same horn made war with the saints, and prevailed against them.' (Dan. vii, *passim*.) These passages, and many others quoted by Protestants as applicable to the Papal Church, show, if they have been rightly applied, that she never was the Church of God, but always the opposite, and the bloodiest enemy of the saints.

"It was argued before the General Assembly by several, and especially by Dr. Rice, that in the days of Luther, 'there was still salt enough in the Church [of Rome] to preserve its existence as a Church of Christ, and the administration of Scriptural ordinances by her officers was valid. But the time came when the voice of God was heard: "Come out of her, my people." The great body of true disciples obeyed the command and came out. Some true disciples no doubt remained, but we can no longer consider the Church of Rome as the Church of Christ.'

"With great deference to the opinion of so able a divine, we must beg leave to protest most earnestly against the sentiment that the Whore of Babylon was ever the Bride, the Lamb's wife! No amount of 'salt' could effect such a wonderful transformation as this! And we most solemnly protest, too, against the doctrine that 'Scriptural ordinances' were ever administered by the Man of Sin and Son of Perdition, and his 'commissioned agents.' They were to do many wonders, according to the Scripture, but no such wonder as this—for they were 'lying wonders,' which 'Scriptural ordinances' are not. Besides, what was the character of the Romish Church before the Almighty called upon his people to come out of her? Let the Scriptures answer: 'Babylon the great is fallen, is fallen, and is become the habitation of devils, and the hold of every foul spirit, and a cage of every unclean and hateful bird. For all nations have drunk of the wine of the wrath of her fornication, and the kings of the earth have committed fornication with her, and the merchants of the earth have waxed rich through the abundance of her delicacies.' (Rev. xviii: 2, 3.)

Throughout the Scriptures, admitting the interpretations of Protestants, the Papal Church is represented as antagonistical to the people of God. They composed no part of her. She is represented as making war with the saints, and overcoming them; as drunk with the blood of God's people; not as making war with and overcoming herself; and as being drunk with her own blood. That God had a people in her bounds is true; and God warns them to get out of those bounds, lest, in destroying her, they should be destroyed; just as Christ warned his disciples to escape from Judea when they saw the abomination of desolation standing where it should not. But the fact that there were true and real saints in the bounds of the Papal Church, could prove nothing; the General Assembly admits that she includes many now. There are many in Germany and elsewhere in her dominions that are now protesting in thunder tones against her corruptions and abominations. Indeed, Dr. Rice has fully answered himself; for, during the same debate, he said: 'The question is not whether any who belong to the Church of Rome are, or may be, truly pious. It is admitted on all hands, that there may be members of that community who are the true children of God; but still they are not members of any branch of the Church of Christ on earth. The validity of baptism does not rest on the piety merely of the person administering, but upon his authority to administer.

"If the piety of a portion of her members can not make mystical Babylon the Church of God now, neither could it before the Reformation. There are many pious people in the United States — more, a great deal, in proportion, than ever belonged at one time to the Romish Church — and yet, the United States is not the Church of God.

"But the General Assembly seemed to think that there was more truth in the Church of Rome before than since the Reformation—that she never became hopelessly corrupt in doctrine until the Council of Trent. This we presume to be a mistake. The Council of Trent but uttered the voice of Papacy in the form of decrees. There was not a sentiment then uttered that had not previously been held by the hierarchy. Let the history of the Romish Church speak. Long before this Council, did she not claim for the Pope the attributes of holiness and infallibility? Did she not assert that she was Christ's vicar upon earth?—Lord God the Pope? Did she not claim for him dominion, temporal and spiritual, over the whole earth;

and declare that he might dispose of crowns, and kingdoms, and continents, at his sovereign pleasure? That he had a right to dethrone kings, absolve subjects from their allegiance, and by his mandate, make that sin which was no sin, and convert sin into virtue? Were not her garments reeking with the blood of God's people? Had she not thrown down the altars, and subverted the worship of God; filling her temples with the images of saints and angels, and establishing the adoration of relics and dead men's bones? Had she not licensed sin by selling indulgences; annulled the doctrine of repentance by her superstitious penances, and that of justification by faith in Jesus, by foolish observances and human merit? In a word, she was stained with every crime, foul with every pollution; had assumed and exercised the most hellish powers; had propagated as divine truths the most outrageous falsehoods; had uttered the most horrid blasphemies, and had filled the world with error, fraud, superstition, and blood! The earth was drunk with the wine of her fornication.

"We have read her history to little purpose if, before the Reformation, the Romish Church was not a more formidable enemy to truth, (we do not say more abominably corrupt,) than she is now. Then her abominations were less disguised. No palliation of them was attempted. Her mien was then more haughty. Kings trembled at her frown. The thunders of the Vatican shook the world. The fires of her persecutions lighted up all lands, and the swords of her crusaders gleamed in all eyes. The blood of martyrs crimsoned the whole earth. 'The world wondered after the beast.' She sat a queen and reigned without a rival. She had almost banished the Word of God from the habitations of men, and crushed to death the few and feeble adherents of the truth. 'Darkness covered the earth, and gross darkness the people.'

"But she is no longer so formidable and so terrible. No kings now tremble at her frown. She has no crowns, and kingdoms, and continents to dispose of. The Vatican now speaks in almost harmless tones, and her mandates are held in derision and contempt by nations and multitudes that once quailed before them as the decrees of destiny. The fires of her persecutions have been extinguished, and her army of crusaders disbanded. Her whole policy has been changed. She has substituted craft and cunning for force and persecution. She supplicates where she once commanded. And, in spite of her opposition, the Bible is being multiplied, and the Gospel preached beyond all example. The army of truth is invading the territories of the Papal Church, and rapidly pressing to her utter overthrow. We appeal to all candid minds—and let them answer in the light of the Bible and of history—if the Romish Church, under Gregory XVI., is not a Church of Christ, was she such a Church under Gregory VII.? Can, in a word, the most tortuous construction of the Scriptures, or the most ingenious application of the '*salt*' of logic, transform the Man of Sin into the Church of God? or the Whore of Babylon into the Bride of the Redeemer?"

From the fatal conclusions of the positions taken by the General Assembly, there is no possible escape. The baptisms and ordinances of all Protestants are nullified, whether Romish baptisms are valid or invalid.

There is one position that might be taken, if one could be found willing to destroy the people's confidence in the Word of God, in the truth of prophecy, in the veracity, faithfulness, and power of Jesus Christ, to save his party organization.

That position is to affirm that the gates of hell had triumphed over the Church of Christ; the last visible Church, that composed his kingdom on earth, had been " given to another people"—had been destroyed from the face of the earth,—and that "the faith" was the *second* time given to the world for another trial with the powers of darkness; that the kingdom set up by the God of heaven—the Church upbuilt by Jesus Christ himself—having yielded to the assaults of hell, Christ divinely commissioned Luther and Calvin, and their coadjutors, to see if they could not do better than he had done, in establishing visible Churches that could stand against the powers of Satan; that Christ commissioned these men, directly, as he did John the Baptist, to preach, and to baptize, and recover the victory, which he had so ignominiously lost, from the hands of Satan!

The man who would say this, would brand the Bible with falsehood, and Christ with imposture, it is true; but what will not man do rather than confess that he is wrong, and has led others into error? It may possibly be thought that no Christian man would advocate, before the Christian world, such a position.

What will the reader say when we inform him that one of the members of that very Assembly did rise upon that floor and urge the Presbyterian Assembly to take this very ground! That man was Professor Thornwell. We quote one paragraph from his speech:

"The Reformers themselves evidently had an extraordinary commission to rebuild the walls of Jerusalem. The towers, bulwarks, and palaces of the city of the great King had fallen into ruins, and they were raised up, in the providence of God, to reconstruct the edifice according to the pattern shown them in the mount. Their authority was not derived from Rome, nor from any of her prelates; the seal of their commission was not the imposition of Episcopal hands, nor the transmission of sacerdotal grace. They were called of God, and derived their authority from Christ; and in consequence of that call and of that authority, the Churches which they formed were as truly Churches of the Redeemer as those which were planted by the hands of the Apostles."

It was well that the General Assembly did not countenance such irreverent utterances,* preferring to peril the ecclesiastical claims of all Protestants, in the eyes of man, and be repudiated, it may be, rather than to assume this attitude toward Christ.

Suppose it were granted that God raised up Luther, and Calvin, and others, to do what his Son had failed to do, did he not inspire them? Did he not deliver "the faith" to them, as he did to the saints at first? Did he leave them to teach for doctrine and for observance whatever they severally saw fit in their own unassisted wisdom to do?—to form visible Churches after patterns not shown in the mount, but after their own devisings?

The position of Professor Thornwell forces him to claim inspiration for the founders of the Reformed Churches. And then, what follows? In what a light is God placed by this assumption, and Christ, also, if he essayed the second time to raise up visible Churches? Did God

---

* Do not Methodists take this very ground with reference to the Wesleys? See their Discipline, page 1.

inspire **Luther** to teach consubstantiation, and Calvin to denounce it as false and impious? Luther to give one form of Church government, and Calvin a different one? and so on through all the variant doctrines and practices of Protestants; until, displeased with these, he raised up Wesley to deny his sovereignty and salvation by grace, without works, as taught by Calvin, Luther, and Paul?

We leave this subject to the serious and prayerful reflection of the reader.

If no baptism be valid except administered by a duly ordained minister of Christ in a true Church of Christ, visible, as the Assembly truly decided, let Presbyterians and the world decide if the baptisms of Luther, John Calvin, John Knox, or any one of the first Presbyterian ministers or members, were valid.

Here is a literal history of the baptism of John Calvin, the father and founder of Presbyterianism. We take it from the columns of an exchange paper:

"THE BAPTISM OF JOHN CALVIN.—John Calvin was born of Papal parents, and received his baptism from a priest of mystical Babylon—a consecrated emissary of 'the man of sin and son of perdition.' While an infant, 'muling and puking in his nurse's arms,' he was taken by his parents or sponsors to the nearest Papal meeting-house, to have his soul regenerated. At the door of the Church he was met by the priest, to denote that as little Calvin was not yet of the number of the faithful, he had no right to enter into that sacred place; and after asking the little fellow what he demanded of the Church, and telling him the conditions on which the demand would be granted, (the parents answering when necessary, in the name of the child,) the priest proceeded to prepare him for the reception of the sacrament of salvation, as follows: 1st. He breathed upon him and said, *Depart from me, thou unclean spirit, and give place to the Holy Ghost, the Comforter.* 2d. He made the sign of the cross upon his forehead. 3d. He put a little blessed salt into the babe's mouth, saying, 'Receive the salt of wisdom; may it be unto thee a propitiation unto everlasting life.' 4th. The priest then proceeded to exorcisms by which, in the name of Jesus Christ, and through the merits of his death upon the cross, (the sign of which he frequently made on little Calvin,) he commanded the devil to depart from the child's soul, and ordered him to give place unto the Holy Ghost.

"By these ceremonies, the infant Calvin being prepared to be admitted into the Church, as one delivered, in a great measure (so his parents believed) from the power of Satan, and belonging to Jesus Christ, the priest permitted him to be brought into that part of the Church where the baptismal font was, saying, '*Enter into the Church of God, that thou mayest have part with Christ unto everlasting life.*' And while proceeding to the font, the old Calvin (for young Calvin) recited with an audible voice, the Apostle's Creed and the Lord's Prayer. Then the priest recited another exorcism, and at the end of it, touched the ears and nostrils of the infant Calvin, with a little spittle, saying, '*Ephpheta,*' that is, '*Be thou opened unto an odor of sweetness; but be thou put to flight, O Devil, for the judgment of God will be at hand.*'

"They were now at the baptismal font. The waters in this font had been solemnly blessed on the eve of Easter and Pentecost, to serve throughout the whole year. In blessing these waters a lighted torch was put into the font, to represent the Divine love, which is communicated to the soul by baptism and the light of good examples, which all who are baptized ought to

DEATH BY THREE HORNS. 49

give, and holy oil and chrism were mixed with the water, to represent the spiritual union of the soul with God, by the grace received by baptism.

"Before these waters were applied to little Calvin, he had to undergo some such examination as the following:

"*Priest.*—What is your name?

"*Little Calvin.*—John Calvin.*

"*Priest.*—John, dost thou renounce the devil and all his works?

"*Little Calvin.*—I do renounce them.

"*Priest.*—Dost thou detest and abhor all the maxims and vanities of the world, which are the pomps of the devil, and abhor all sins which are his works?

"*Little Calvin.*—I detest and abhor them all.

"*Priest.*—Dost thou believe in God, the Father, Almighty, the maker of heaven and earth?

"*Little Calvin.*—I do believe.

"*Priest.*—Dost thou believe in Jesus Christ, his only Son, our Lord, who was born and suffered death?

"*Little Calvin.*—I do believe.

---

* As little Calvin was only a few hours or days old, of course he spoke this through his godfather.

"*Priest.*—Dost thou believe in the Holy Ghost, the Holy Catholic Church, the communion of saints, the resurrection of the body, and life eternal?

"*Little Calvin.*—I do believe.

"*Priest.*—John, do you desire to be baptized?

"*Little Calvin.*—I do desire it.

"Then the priest anointed him with holy oil on the breast and between the shoulders, making the sign of the cross and saying, 'I anoint thee with the oil of salvation, in Christ Jesus our Lord, that thou mayest have life everlasting." The father then held the babe, bareheaded, over the font, the priest poured the greasy water, consecrated as afore written, into the child's face, in the name of the Trinity.

"Little Calvin was thus *made a Christian,* and was immediately anointed on the crown of the head with holy chrism, to signify that royal priesthood to which he was raised by baptism. He was clothed with a white garment, as an emblem of the spotless innocence with which his soul was adorned; and a lighted torch was put into his hand as an emblem of a good example.

"Thus John Calvin, (who, if he had not come, Presbyterianism had not been,) was initiated into the Christian Church and made a child of God and an heir of glory by baptism!

"The Old School General Assembly of the Presbyterian Church in the United States, a few years ago, decided that no baptism was valid except administered by a regular ordained minister in the true Church of God, visible; that the Romish Church was not the Church of God at all, and that, therefore, baptism administered within its pales and by its priesthood was no baptism! Then, according to Presbyterian principles, John Calvin, Theodore Beza, John Knox, and their cotemporary Reformers, all of whom were baptized by Papists, had no Christian baptism! The chain of baptismal successors from the Apostolic Church to the Presbyterian Church, which the General Assembly had declared to be essential to valid baptism, has been broken asunder, and all the spiritual smiths beneath the skies can not mend it. And thus our Presbyterian brethren, by the solemn decision of their highest ecclesiastical tribunal, have no baptism!"

CHAPTER III.

The Question in the New School Presbyterian General Assembly, 1854—Reports of Speeches, etc—The Tri-lemma.

ON the year 1854, this question came up for discussion in the New School General Assembly, and was discussed for two days or more. It was a practical question, since the sessions of one or more of their societies had received members upon their Romish baptisms, and one Mr. Riley, who had been so received, had been, for some time, a minister among them, and had baptized not a few infants and adults.

We have used great industry to obtain as full a report of the discussion and speeches as possible, from the most authentic sources, religious and secular.

The following Reports, which appeared at the time in the columns of the New York Observer, the organ of the N. S. Presbyterians, can be relied upon, so far as they go. There were certain sentiments advanced by distinguished doctors of divinity that the editors of the Observer did not wish for their lay readers to see, lest their fears should be alarmed.

For instance, we may suppose that Mr. Riley, in substance, said, when he moved that it was inexpedient for the Assembly to express an opinion on the subject:

"Mr. President, how can this Assembly decide that the baptisms received by the priests of Rome are invalid, and save the ecclesiastical existence of Presbyterian Churches? How many have been received from that communion, since Presbyterianism commenced, in the sixteenth century, upon their Romish baptisms, that have become ministers, and have baptized scores of other ministers, and thousands of members. What will you do with all these ministers, and with those whom they have baptized, if you decide this question negatively? I, myself, sir, have received no other than Romish baptism, and was received among you upon it, and I am, to-day, satisfied with it. Will this Assembly nullify it by an *ex post facto* law? If this Report is adopted, you will nullify it, and declare me unbaptized. What will you do with me? exclude me, or re-baptize me? To be consistent, you must demand my re-baptism, and all those I have baptized since I have been a minister among you, and you must pursue this course with all those among you, who have either been baptized by Romish priests, or who have been baptized by those ministers who have been so baptized; and where will you stop sir?—where will you stop? Can you tell? I can tell you where you will have to *begin*—with Calvin, and Zwingle, and Beza, and Knox, and all the first Presbyterian ministers, and re-baptize them, and all whom they baptized, and so on down to the present. I said I was satisfied with my baptism, though it was administered by a priest of Rome, and I expect to be so long as I am a Protestant; for why should I not be? Who of you, what Presbyterian minister in the United States, can give me a more valid one? You will not say,—no Presbyterian will say,— that your own Calvin was not validly baptized! I was baptized in the *same Church*, and by the *same minister*—a ROMISH PRIEST!! The baptisms and ordinances of all Presbyterian ministers are from Romish priests indirectly—mine, *directly*. If my worthy compeers around me were baptized in the remote streams, I can claim to have received it at the pure fountain-head!"

Such, we suppose, was substantially the speech of Mr. Riley, from the meager outlines we have been able to gather.

We submit the Reports as published in the New York Observer.

"*Extract from Report of Proceedings of Presbyterian General Assembly, held at Philadelphia, Pa., May* 18–30, 1854, *as reported in New York Observer:*

"*Monday Morning, May* 22.—The Committee on Romish Baptism, through its Chairman, Dr. Hatfield, reported, recommending that the General Assembly declare that, in their opinion, baptism in the Roman Catholic Church is not to be regarded as Christian baptism. This Report is signed by Revs. Drs. Hatfield and Cox.

"The Rev. Henry B. Smith, D.D., of Union Theological Seminary, made a Minority Report, That it is inexpedient for the Assembly to decide that [such] baptism is necessarily invalid.

"We here reserve these Reports, not being able to insert them here.

"Rev. Dr. Barnes moved, that it is inexpedient for this Assembly to decide Romish baptism necessarily invalid.

"Rev. Mr. Niles, of Michigan, moved the indefinite postponement of the subject. This was seconded by Dr. Allen. The motion was lost.

"At this point of the debate, the order of the day was taken up, etc.

"*Monday Afternoon.*—The Report of the majority of the Committee on Romish Baptism was taken up. The Rev. Mr. Dobie read the definitions of baptism as given in Roman Catholic catechisms, to show that there can be no relation between our doctrine and that of the Romish Church.

"Rev. Mr. Riley offered the following Resolution, viz.:

"'That in view of the great diversity of opinions, and of practice in the Presbyterian Church, on the subject of Popish baptism, and in view of the previous action of the Assembly, it may be inexpedient for the present Assembly to take action in the case.'

"Dr. Brainerd advocated this amendment, and showed the difficulties of taking either Report as the dogmatic assertion of a doctrine. For instance, if you say Romish baptism is valid, your converts from Rome will sometimes constrain your conscience by asserting that, in their estimation, Romish sacraments are valid. If you say that Romish baptism is invalid, you will excite prejudice in the minds of Catholics, which will prevent your making such advancement toward their conversion as you desire.

" Rev. Mr. Clapp said there might be pious persons in the Papal Church. Now, suppose such a parent in that faith has his child baptized, and twenty years after, that child is converted, will you re-baptize him, when he had been consecrated to God in the rite of baptism in faith? We can not pass an absolute rule such as the Majority Report lays down.

" Hon. Mr. Taylor urged the adoption of the Majority Report in a speech of great earnestness.

" Rev. Mr. LeDoux would have this Assembly leave the subject with the pastors and sessions of the Churches to decide each case as it arises. He hoped Mr. Riley's resolution might pass, as any more stringent rule will embarrass our Church.

" Dr. Beman said : The opponents of the Report which I sustain may be divided into three strata, (I do not mean to call my opponents fossils—I mean as a mere figure of speech.) The upper stratum considers Rome as a Christian

Church, and her ministers as ministers of Christ. The middle stratum holds that it is not a Church, and that its ministers are not ministers of Christ but, as laymen, men and women, may, in extreme cases, administer baptism, therefore Romish baptism is valid. Mr. Beman said there was no such extreme case which can be named. If I may guess what is an extreme case in their estimation, I should say that it means that a child is likely to die before an ordained minister can get there. If this be what is meant, we are on the ground of baptismal regeneration, and on the way to Rome. As for those cases in which some converted Catholics stand by their Romish baptism, no one supposes that they need be affected. There may be exceptions, but in this case we are called to make a declaration of sentiment. The lower stratum contains those who agree, in the main, with the Report; and as, in the physical world, the lower stratum is so hard pressed that its original features are lost, so with these men: they are pressed so hard, that you find nothing distinctive about them. This is a sort of dough-faced operation, into which I will not enter. Let us adopt one Report or the other. Our standards favor the Report, and I am not afraid, as a Presbyterian, of these standards. They declare the Pope to be Antichrist, and that his ministers must be excluded from the Christian ministry. Let us not shrink from the conclusion which flows from this principle. The Scriptures have decided this thing. Rome is the scarlet harlot riding on the beast with seven heads and ten horns. We have some Presbyterians who crave to lay a pillow under her old aching head, which is about to be scathed with the thunderbolts of the Almighty! Kind nurses are they!—very sisters of charity! This Church is drunk with the blood of saints, and yet there are some who advocate the validity of a baptism administered by men whose hands are dripping with the blood of the saints. As for offending the Catholics, it will not produce this result. It will be with them as with a converted Catholic woman I know of, who, on being asked if she wished to be baptized, replied: 'I certainly do. I wish to have the last mark of the beast washed off.' Mr. Beman hoped we would pass the Report of the Committee, as being in accordance with our standards, our Bible, and with the wants of the age.

"*Tuesday Morning, May* 23.— * * * The unfinished business of yesterday was resumed, viz.: the consideration of Mr. Riley's amendment to the motion to adopt the Report of the Committee on Romish Baptism.

"Dr. James C. Fisher strongly advocated the entire repudiation of Romish baptism, and in support of this, recited the definition of baptism as given in the standards of our Church. He said the question turns on this: Is the Papal Church in any sense a Christian Church? Our standards denounced it as Antichrist.

"Dr. Riddle made a happy reply to the ridicule of Dr. Beman, yesterday, and protested against the disposition to bring up hypothetical cases to have a deliverance by the General Assembly *in thesê*. This is not in accordance with the analogies of our Supreme Court. It is a pure question of abstraction, not brought upon an actual case, where matters of discipline are involved. We are called on to decide whether it is expedient to declare that Popish baptism is necessarily invalid, and not whether the Pope is thus or so, and whether the Papal Church is a Christian Church or not. At considerable length, Dr. Riddle argued against the expediency of making any deliverance on this point. If made, it would not satisfy many consciences. Not only is the General Assembly divided, but there is the same diversity in the Church at large.

"Rev. Mr. Boardman said that it was not a question *in thesê*, but a practical question. Our business is to affirm or deny the sentiments of that Report; and it is expedient for us to affirm with emphasis, the invalidity of baptism administered by the man of sin. There are three questions which will guide my vote: 1. Is the Romish Church a true Church? 2. If it be a true Church, is the baptism administered by it valid? 3. Is lay baptism valid? These points Mr. Boardman argued at some length for the purpose of sustaining his views in favor of the Majority Report.

"Rev. J. G. King said it was the desire of many of the younger pastors, 'Junior Patriarchs,' as they had been facetiously called, to have this question discussed. They wanted the advice and counsel of this body. They have to deal with this question in a practical manner.

"Dr. Franklin Knox, of San Francisco, said, we have no right to consume time in discussing whether the Roman Church is a Christian Church. There are practical difficulties connected with this subject, and if you adopt an iron rule (I would call it a Papal rule) you will do mischief.

"Rev. Mr. Snyder, in an admirable strain, advocated the inexpediency of passing the Majority Report, not because he did not believe it to be true, but because he did not believe he had any right to force his inferences on those who differed from him.

"Rev. Mr. Waterbury moved that a committee of three be appointed, to which should be referred the whole business.

"Dr. Beman would second the motion with a single modification: that both the papers shall be referred to the same committee, with the addition of two members of this body, with instructions to report at the next Assembly.

"Mr. Waterbury accepted the suggestion of Dr. Beman.

"Rev. J. G. King called for a division on the question.

"Dr. Brainerd was in favor of the commitment, and was delighted that we had reached such a termination. We express a general principle, and yet preserve the rights of conscience.

"Rev. Mr. Sherwood was opposed to the motion, because many had not expressed their sentiments, and because, also, no good can be secured. The next Assembly will have to travel over the same ground. We ought to settle the question at this meeting of the Assembly.

"At this point the hour of adjournment arrested the discussion.

"*Tuesday Afternoon.*—The motion of Mr. Waterbury to refer the Reports on Romish baptism to a committee to report to the next Assembly, was taken up.

"Dr. Spear opposed the motion. He wished the Assembly to distinctly vote that they can lay down no general law to bind others in this matter. We can fix no rule on this point; Dr. Beman himself acknowledged there were exceptional cases.

"At this point Mr. Waterbury asked leave to withdraw his motion of commitment, and it was granted.

"The original amendment of Mr. Riley was then taken up. The discussion was suspended at this point, to take up the order of the day, etc.

"*Tuesday, May* 30.—The subject of Popish baptism was indefinitely postponed."

The following corroborating, and in some cases, fuller reports, are from the columns of the *New York Daily Times:*

PRESBYTERIAN GENERAL ASSEMBLY — NEW SCHOOL.

"PHILADELPHIA, Monday, May 22, 1854.

"This reverend body has occupied itself this morning with several grave and exciting subjects. After a Report commending the Union Theological Seminary in New York, and the Lane Seminary at Cincinnati, and speaking encouragingly of the projected Seminary at Galena, two Reports, majority and minority, were presented from a committee previously appointed, to consider the question—*Is the Baptism of the Romish Church valid?* The Majority Report, signed by Revs. Drs. Hatfield and Cox, took ground against the validity of such baptism. It argued from previous decisions of the Assembly; from the Confession of Faith; from the acknowledged apostasy of the Romish Church; and from consistency. As the Church of Rome was Antichrist, she was not to be recognized as a Christian body, nor her priesthood to be regarded as a Christian ministry. All its other sacraments are universally repudiated by Protestant Churches; there was no reason why this should not also be. The Report concluded with these words:

"'Planting ourselves on the broad and firm ground of a Protestant and a pure Christianity, and believing that the circumstances of the Church and of the age demand of us a manly and unambiguous avowal of our faith in relation to the pretensions and abominations of this "Mystery of Iniquity," this General Assembly solemnly declare their conviction that the ministers of the Church of Rome are not authorized to administer the sacraments ordained by Christ our Lord in the Gospel; and that the administration of what is denominated baptism in the Roman Catholic Church, is not to be recognized as Christian baptism.'

"Rev. Dr. Smith, of the Union Theological Seminary, presented a Minority Report, which was read by the Moderator. It argued that it was inexpedient for the Assembly to decide that baptism in the Roman Catholic Church is necessarily invalid. A presumptive argument was to be found in the unanimous consent of the Reformed Churches and theologians. The French, Dutch, German, and English Churches; the great Reformers, divines like CALVIN, TURRETIN, and HOOKER, admit the validity of Romish baptisms, while contending against the corruptions of the Papacy. During the century of the Reformation, only the Anabaptists, of all the sects of the Reformers, advocated the contrary opinion. With the exception of the Old School Presbyterian Church, no considerable Protestant body in this country has taken the position that Romish baptism is necessarily invalid; and against that, the Princeton *Repertory*, the great Review of the Church, took ground. The Assembly ought not to decide against such a current of testimony, except on the strongest grounds.

"It argued further, that baptism, like marriage, may be valid, even when the form of it is irregular. Even those Churches which insist most strenuously on sacramental grace, allow the validity of lay baptism in certain cases. It also distinguished between the Roman Catholic Church and the Papacy: because the latter was corrupt and Antichrist, does not prove that the former has none of the elements of a true Christian Church. Even a ministry is not essential to the being of a Church; and even in a corrupt Church there may be a lawful ministry. As the Roman Catholic Church, in its public confessions, retains Christian truth on fundamental doctrines, as the Trinity and the necessity of grace, though intermingled and overlaid with errors, superinduced by the Papal and sacramental systems, it is still to be regarded as a Church, and its ministry lawful, despite its apostasy, and the sacrament of baptism as administered therein may be held to be valid. The Report also argued the inexpediency of taking ground against the validity of such baptism, on the ground of consistency, and the relations of the Church to Roman Catholics in this country.

"On the perusal of the two Reports, a lively debate sprang up, which elicited a variety of opinions. Some were for postponing it, in order to have time to prepare for a regular discussion of it; others were for a discussion now; others still agreed with the advice of Professor Smith's Report, that the Assembly take no ground on the subject. It transpired in the debate, that two of the clergymen of the body were converted Roman Catholics, one of whom had been re-baptized and the other not. Both now agreed that there was no good ground for denying the validity of Romish baptisms; because it is not to be assumed that the Romish Church is not a Christian Church, and because the real validity of baptism depends upon the intent and design of the subject of it much more than upon the regularity of its form. Some of the oldest and ablest men of the Assembly expressed themselves on one side or the other, very definitely: Dr. Beman warmly espousing the Majority Report; Mr. Barnes and Dr. Spear the opposite. No conclusion was reached before the order of the day arrived, and it is therefore to come up again.

"PHILADELPHIA, Tuesday, May 23, 1854.

"The subject of Romish baptism came up again in the afternoon, and drew forth a few strong speeches.

"Mr. Dobie read extracts from the Romish Catechism, to show the radical difference between the baptism of that Church and the baptism of the New Testament.

"Rev. Mr. Riley proposed to substitute a minute, declaring the inexpediency of any action on the subject. [See his position on page 56.]

"Dr. Brainerd also thought it inexpedient to legislate on the subject. It was not good policy to do anything to estrange us from Catholics. To make a violent assault upon their rites or their character, as a Church, would be just what the priests of that Church would like. Moreover, the subject is invested with great difficulty. IF THE VALIDITY OF CATHOLIC BAPTISM BE DENIED, THEN LUTHER AND CALVIN, FROM WHOM OUR BAPTISM IS DERIVED, WERE UNBAPTIZED; AND TO MAINTAIN OUR OWN STANDING IN THE CHURCH, WE MUST BAPTIZE THE ASHES OF THE REFORMERS!! Questions like this, involving matters of conscience, can not be settled by majorities. The discussion would do good, but the Assembly should be slow to legislate.

"Rev. Mr. Clapp thought the adoption of the Majority Report—which declares the invalidity of Romish baptism—WOULD LEAD TO PRACTICAL DIFFICULTY. What if the child of sincerely pious parents within the pale of the Catholic

Church should present himself for admission to a Protestant Church? To require his rebaptism would be to deny the faith and sincerity of his parents. He opposed any such declaration, because the validity of any rite depends much more upon the intent and spirit of him who receives it than on the character of him who administers it; and because it would be attaching too much importance to the form, and too little to the substance, of the ordinance.

"Hon. Elisha Taylor, of Cleveland, strongly advocated the invalidity of Romish baptism. Baptism, as defined by the New Testament, WAS AN INITIATORY ORDINANCE; IF SO, IT COULD RIGHTFULLY BE PERFORMED ONLY BY THOSE BELONGING TO THE CHURCH INTO WHICH IT ADMITTED THE SUBJECT. The question was not as to the intent of the subject, but as to the authority of the administrator. A few years ago a company of infidels in New-York admitted their members by the rite of baptism, in derision of Christianity. What if any one had received this baptism innocently, and with good intentions, would it have been valid baptism? The hierarchy of Rome were as corrupt and as hostile to true Christianity as this band of infidels; and any principle which would admit the validity of their baptism would sanctify the mockery of the infidels. He was for speaking out on the subject. There was quite too much disposition to trim and compromise for the sake of effect. This is no question of policy; and if it were, he knew of no better policy than to declare the truth boldly.

"Rev. Mr. LeDoux repeated his opinion that the Romish Church was a true Church of Christ, though greatly corrupted. Any just definition of a Church would necessarily include the Romish communion.

"Rev. Dr. Beman made a powerful speech in opposition to the Minority Report, in which logic and wit were finely intermingled. He divided the friends of the Minority Report into three strata—not intending, he said, to imply by that term that they were fossils. The upper stratum believed in the genuine Christian character of the Romish Church; they are opposed to telling the truth on the subject, because they did not believe it. The second stratum believed that baptism was valid by whomsoever administered—by laymen or women. The third believed in the principle of the Majority Report, but like the lower strata in the physical world, were pressed down flat, and were for quiet. They were opposed to action in any shape, for policy's sake. These several classes were held up to ridicule, and reasoned against in a manner that kept up a lively interest. Dr. Beman has but few superiors as a debater. Deliberate, shrewd, witty, and unmerciful, he makes the worst kind of a foe; and generally marches off the field in triumph, if not stained with the blood and brains of his adversaries. His speech on this occasion disclosed not a little of the vigor of his best days.

"PHILADELPHIA, Tuesday, May 30.
"The Presbyterian General Assembly (New School) adjourned *sine die* this afternoon.
"The subject of Popish baptism was indefinitely postponed."

Thus closed the discussion of this vexed question, to be brought up henceforth, not once in a decade of years, but yearly, if the query will be entertained from their societies.

The reader will see that it is one question that Protestants can not answer, and save their ecclesiastical existences. The General Assembly confessed itself in a *di*lemma, but we should say it was in a *tri*-lemma. Its dilemma was this:

If it decided that baptisms, at the hands of the priests of Rome, are *invalid*, then they would destroy their own baptisms, and those of all Protestant sects, because the fathers and founders, and all the first Pedobaptist ministers, received their baptisms in the corrupt Church of Rome, and at the hands of her priests.

If they should decide that the baptisms of Romish priests are valid, they would also destroy the validity of their own, as well as those of all Protestants, because the General Assembly would thereby declare the Church of Rome to be a true Church of Christ visible; which, if she is, Pedobaptist societies are *schismatics*, and excommunicated parties, and no Churches, and consequently their ministers are unordained, and unbaptized, and without authority either to preach or to baptize as Gospel ministers. So it is fatal to them, decide it either way.

The *Tri*-lemma is the middle horn: the confession of the General Assembly of its inability to decide whether its own ministers are baptized, or have authority to baptize, and, consequently, whether their societies are visible Churches of Christ!

We should think, for the General Assembly to

rest impaled upon this middle horn, would be as fatal as either of the others.

What! can not Presbyterian ministers, with all their boasted learning, decide among themselves whether they have received Christian baptism? Can they not tell the world, when convened in their great Assembly, whether they be duly ordained and baptized ministers of Christ or not? Can they not tell the world whether their societies are visible Churches of Christ? Did Presbyterian ministers return from their General Assembly, and confess to their people that they were lost in thick darkness, not being able to decide whether they or their members were properly baptized, or members, in reality, of visible Churches? This was their real situation; but we have not heard of one minister making such a confession to his people. Our impression is that all have agreed to keep their people in the dark about the whole matter. We have heard of their denying, stoutly, that such a question was ever mooted, and that the Assembly was unable to answer. We do not believe that one Presbyterian lay member, in one hundred,

7

if one in one thousand, ever heard of it. They are in the profoundest ignorance of the fatal *tri-lemma* in which they are placed.

Would it not have been the part of conscientious Christian men, when they saw their situation as Protestants, as they did see it in the light of the powerful discussions of that General Assembly, when they returned to their flocks, to have called them together, and frankly confessed the case to them, and told them: "You must excuse us from preaching longer to you as *ministers*, or baptizing any more, or administering the Supper to you, for we can not see that we have authority to do so, having received only Romish baptisms, and you are not qualified to receive it, not being baptized by other than Romish priests, yourselves, indirectly. You must excuse us from all official duties until this vital question is settled?"

Now, when all these facts shall have been made known to Presbyterians, and to all Pedobaptist sects, what should an intelligent and conscientious membership do, but to wait upon their ministers, *en masse*, and say to them, "Gentlemen, we have learned, through other sources than yourselves, that you have acknowledged yourselves unable to decide whether you are duly baptized and ordained ministers of the Church of Christ, visible; unable to decide that we, your members, are baptized, or members, in fact, of a visible Church. That we have been deceived by you, *intentionally*, hitherto, we do not charge; but you certainly do not wish to deceive henceforward, our children, and the world, intentionally, for you now see the position you occupy. Suspend your ministerial functions, preach no more as ministers, baptize no more, and introduce no more into our societies as valid Churches, until this question is satisfactorily settled: *Whether the baptisms of Romish priests are valid,* or whether Pedobaptist ministers can administer more valid baptism than Roman Catholic priests?"

Ought not all the Presbyterian membership in this land to unite in one huge petition—*instar montis*—of mountainous proportions, and roll it into the presence of the next General Assembly, calling upon it to answer, if they and their children have been baptized, and are really members of Christ's visible Church.

What position should the public take—men of the world who are appealed to to support and attend upon the ministrations of Presbyterian and Pedobaptist ministers and "Churches?" Should they not say: "You must excuse us, if we withhold our usual support and countenance, until this, to us, very important question is, to our minds, satisfactorily answered. If you be only Romish priests in fact, having no better ordinances than they to give to our wives and our children, then we do not wish them to receive ordinances at your hands. When you introduce them into your societies, they honestly suppose they are members of the Church of Christ, which your own General Assembly declares your societies are not, if the Romish Church is not a visible Church of Christ; and, in fact, are much less Churches, if the Romish Church is now, or was, in the days of Luther, a Church of Christ visible! We have no use for the baptisms of Catholic priests, nor for the Roman Catholic Church as a religious body, and wish purer ordinances for our families, whose guardians we are, and must therefore decline yours.

BAPTISTS need not be reminded of their duty in this case. Shall we be so kind as to step in and decide this matter for Presbyterians and Pedobaptists? Shall we, by our *acts*, say to them, and to the world that is watching us, we regard those men baptized and duly-ordained ministers in true Churches of Christ? Do we believe they have received valid baptism? Do we believe that their societies, originated and set up, not by the God of heaven, built, not by Christ, but by Luther, and Calvin, and Wesley, are Scriptural Churches, or Christian Churches in any sense? Do we believe it, or believe that their ministers possess the proper qualifications to carry out the commission of the Son of God— *i. e.*, preach, baptize, administer the Supper, etc.? Baptists do not. No intelligent and true Baptist can; and therefore they can not say so by their *acts*—associating with them as with properly-qualified ministers of Christ. If they preached the faith, in all respects, that was once delivered to the saints, we could not treat them as men qualified to preach as Christ's ministers; and how much less when we believe that they preach contrary to, and in subversion of the doctrines and ordinances of Christ, and would, if left alone, in one generation, obliterate from the world the last trace of the Church he established. Their organizations are rivals against the Church Christ set up, and their teaching is another gospel; and from all such, though they be angels from heaven, we are to withdraw—are to have no company with them, that they may be reproved and ashamed, and the world be warned.

How Presbyterian ministers, or members who have a knowledge of these facts, can presume, in the face of these things, to demand of Baptists to recognize and treat them as ministers, by inviting them into our pulpits to preach, as we only do qualified ministers, and to commune with them as baptized persons, and to acknowledge and treat them as evangelical Churches, is passing strange to us!

They all say their creeds and confessions teach that none are entitled to the Lord's Supper, or ought to be invited to partake of it, unless duly baptized; if there is any doubt about the matter, the Supper should not be offered until the doubt was removed; and yet, they confess to us, through their General Assembly, that they can not tell whether they, themselves, any one of them, have been duly baptized; ay, more, confess that they are not baptized, having received their baptisms from the Man of Sin and the Mother of Harlots.

We think that the action of the General Assembly forever settles the vexed question of open communion.

Anabaptists never did commune with Rome, or those who received her baptisms. The Baptists of to-day are the descendants of the Anabaptists who have, for so many centuries, witnessed for Christ, against the corruptions of Antichrist.

We leave the question with the Protestants of this age to answer, if they can, and preserve their ecclesiastical existences:

ARE THE BAPTISMS OF THE PAPAL HIERARCHY VALID BAPTISMS.

CHAPTER IV.

TWO OTHER QUESTIONS.

Can Protestants oppose the Papacy without being slain by the Papacy? Can Baptists oppose the Papacy without destroying Protestants?

TAKE the negative of both questions. How can two unite to war, except they be agreed? They are violently antagonistic. They hate each other with a cruel hatred, scarcely less than they differ from and hate Baptists. Episcopalians are opposed by Presbyterians and Methodists; while Episcopalians and Presbyterians unite in making war upon Methodists. Old and New School Presbyterians and Congregationalists are each seeking the overthrow and annihilation of the other, and still, like Pilate and Herod, they will all unite in a league of amity and friendship, to oppose the influence of Baptists, either in seeking the salvation of sinners, or the dissemination of their principles.

Talk about all these uniting in *open communion* at the Lord's table, in token of Church and Christian fellowship! What *impious hypocrisy*, what a solemn *mockery*—a *blasphemous farce*, to thus prostitute the holy emblems to the propagation of a *falsehood?* We say Protestants are engaged in a fierce and deadly conflict among themselves, to annihilate each other; how, then, can they unite against Popery?

But could they unite, wherein can they judge the Catholics, without condemning, also, themselves? What principle of Papacy, save that of idolatry, can they attack without their blows recoiling most fearfully upon their own systems and practices?

1. *Will they deny that the Roman Catholic Church is a Scriptural Church, and denounce her as the " Mystery of Iniquity," " The Woman dressed in scarlet, the Mother of Harlots and abominations of the earth?"*

Can not Rome justly say: "Spare me, my *dear children*, and honor your mother, if you would be respected. Do you not all call yourselves *Protestants* and *Reformed?* You then admit yourselves once to have been a *part of myself*, and to have proceeded forth from me! Do you not, to-day, call yourselves 'branches of THE CHURCH?' Of what Church are you branches, but of the HOLY ROMAN CATHOLIC, in which you all acknowledge you originated, and from which, as a branch from a parent trunk, you confessedly proceed? If I, the Catholic Church, am the *mother* of '*harlots*,' and '*abominations*' of the earth, you are all my *children*, and consequently are THOSE VERY HARLOTS AND ABOMINATIONS! You do not well, my daughters, thus to cast reproach upon your *parentage*. I commend to you the example and filialness of your sister, my *favorite* child, the Episcopal Church, which, like a prodigal, is returning to her mother's house."

Could not Rome thus cause the well-aimed blow to recoil upon her Protestant children,[*] for they are her legitimate offspring; and if she is the mother of abominations and harlots, Protest-

---

[*] Baptists are not Protestants, having never belonged to the Catholic Church, more than to-day. "Baptists," said Sir Isaac Newton, "are the only people that never symbolized with Popery."

ants are they. If the fountain is corrupt, all the waters that flow from it are also corrupt. If the Church of Rome is an illegitimate Church, they are illegitimate Churches also. "Either make the tree good, and its fruit good, or else make the tree corrupt, and its fruit corrupt"— (Matt. vii : 23)—is a principle established by the Great Teacher.

2. *Will they deny her the age she claims— that she was founded by Peter, and once presided over by him and preserved against the gates of hell?*

They must do this, else Rome stands forth a Christian and apostolic Church, and besides her there is none other. But they deny her claims, and charge her with being, from the days of Paul, that spirit of *Antichrist* that worked in the early Churches, corrupting Christianity; that it was early repudiated by all the pure Churches; that Popery had no existence in its present form until established by Hilderbrand, A. D. 606; that no Church, similar to the Roman Catholic, was instituted by Christ or his apostles, or existed within six hundred years of their day; and, moreover, all the teachings of the Scriptures positively forbid the idea of such a monstrous system.

Can not Rome reply, "My dear children, do you not see that you commit suicide by taking such a position to discredit *my claims!* You can not, with the least regard to reason, believe that such systems as yours existed in the days of the Apostles, surely, each radically differing from, and destructive of, the other! Did Paul found an *Episcopal* Church at Antioch, a *Presbyterian* Church at Ephesus, and a *Methodist* one at Philippi? Certainly not. All the Churches that were founded in the Apostles' times, were one and identical in *doctrine*, in *organization*, ordinances, and practices. But you do not even claim that you existed in the days of the Apostles, or were founded by them. I know the parentage of each of you, and *beheld you when you were born.* You, my most dutiful Church of England, are the offspring of my wayward and licentious boy, Henry VIII., who was led astray by the love of the beautiful Ann Boleyn, A. D. 1534.

" You, my Lutheran daughter, by the bold and impetuous Martin Luther, A. D. 1525.

" You, my Presbyterian daughter, by the stern and austere Calvin, A. D. 1541 ; while I acknowledge you, dear Methodists, being all the children of Wesley, by the Church of England, (A. D. 1784,) as my legitimate and worthy *grandchildren*, and though quite too noisy and fanatical, yet I can not but be quite partial to you, since, next to your mother, the Church of England, you possess nearly all my features; indeed, the *likeness* is striking and remarkable!"

3. *Will Protestants charge the Church of Rome with being* " *mystical Babylon,*" *and that* " *scarlet woman,*" *drunken with the blood of the saints ?*

May not Rome reply: " If I am BABYLON, because I have persecuted and shed the blood of the heretical Anabaptists, then do *you also belong to Babylon*, for which one of you all have not imbued your hands in their blood? *Your own garments* are scarlet and blood-dyed, as well as my own! It becomes us to keep these *family matters* among ourselves, and not charge each other before our enemies."*

4. *Will Protestants denounce Rome for the iniquitous and blasphemous assumptions of her clergy of the "Divine right" to legislate for the Church of Christ, to make, change, or abolish, rites and ceremonies, etc.?*

Do not Protestants claim the same ANTICHRISTIAN POWERS? See Methodist Discipline, Art. xxii: "Every particular Church may *ordain, change,* or *abolish* rites and ceremonies, so that all things be done to edification"—of whom? The rulers or the judges, of course. They, then, claim to ordain or institute, change and abolish until they are themselves perfectly suited, pleased, and satisfied! Is not this claiming *Antichristian powers?* Does the Pope claim more power?

CALVIN says: "From the beginning the Church has freely allowed herself, excepting the substance, to have rites a little *dissimilar,* for

---

*Read Rev. xviii: 24: "The blood of all the saints is to be found in Babylon." If Protestants also have shed the blood of saints, are they not a part of mystical Babylon?

some immerse *thrice*, and others only *once;*" and he therefore abolished immersion altogether, as inconvenient, and ordained sprinkling in the room of Christ's appointment. He had as good a right to have forbidden baptism entirely, as to change its action in the least. He did abolish *Christian* baptism, and substituted *clerical* baptism instead of it.

5. *Will Protestants declare before the world, that the ordinances administered by the Priests of Rome are invalid, since Rome is no Church, but Antichrist, and her priests therefore the ministers of Antichrist?*

Can not Rome reply: "It is quite unfortunate for you to say so, since you unbaptize Luther and Calvin, and all your first ministers, and thereby acknowledge yourselves unbaptized, and without authority to baptize. If you are not concerned for my honor, you should be for that of those whom you boast of as your ecclesiastical fathers and founders. The less you say about my *baptisms* and *ordinances* the better."

[Presbyterian to Episcopalian, aside: "*It would be as fatal to us to admit her to be the true Church of Christ; for, if so, all we Protestants are evidently schismatics and heretics, and we have been excommunicated from, and anathematized by, her; and, therefore, if she is a true Church, we are no Churches, but in rebellion to Christ. What shall we say?"*]

The dilemma presented by the Archbishop of York to the British Parliament, early as 1558, vaunting itself upon its orthodoxy and succession apostolic, is worthy of special attention just here, and it will show that Presbyterians are not alone between two horns, and impaled upon a third! Here it is:

"The Romish Church is either a true Church, or a false one.

"If *true*, then the Church of England—we may add, all Protestants and Reformed Churches, are schismatics, and have been excommunicated.

"If *false*, then the English Episcopal clergy, and all Protestant ministers, have false orders, are unordained, and without authority to administer the ordinances."

The Parliament heard this with no little *vexation*, saw the fatal *dilemma* in which Protestants were placed, but could not make an election of its horns. It left the question undecided, and left the Romish priests to enjoy a decided triumph. That victory Rome can ever win in conflict with her children.

How can Baptists deny the validity of the ordinances of the Romish Church, without thereby destroying Protestant baptisms and ordinations?

6. *Will Protestants protest against the unscriptural orders of the Catholic clergy, since Christ made all his ministers equal, and only one order?*

But the advocates of Episcopacy, whether Protestant or Methodist, have their three *orders* at least, and their *inferior* and *superior* ministers.

7. *Will they protest against the irreligious practice of the inferior Catholic clergy, of being solemnly sworn to obey reverently in all things the superior clergy?*

The Methodist and Episcopal inferior clergy are compelled to do the same thing! *See Office for Ordination of Deacons and Elders in their Prayer Book and Discipline.* Here is the oath

Catholic Priests are bound to take before they are empowered by the Pope, or their chief ministers, to administer the sacrament of the Church:

THE OATH OF A ROMAN CATHOLIC PRIEST.

"I. N., elect of the Church of N., from henceforward, will be faithful and obedient to St. Peter, the Apostle, and to the holy Roman Church, and to our Lord, the Lord N., and to his successors canonically coming in. I will neither advise, consent, nor do anything that they may lose life or member, or that their persons may be seized, or hands anywise laid upon them, or any injuries offered to them, under any pretense whatsoever. The counsel which they shall intrust me withal, by themselves, their messengers. or letters, I will not, knowingly, reveal to any, to their prejudice. I will help them to defend and keep the Roman Papacy, and the royalties of St. Peter, saving my order against all men. The Legate of the Apostolic See going and coming, I will honorably treat and help in his necessities. The rights, honors, privileges, and authority of the holy Roman Church, of OUR LORD THE POPE, and his aforesaid successors, I will endeavor to preserve, defend, increase, and advance. I will not be in any council, action, or treaty, in which shall be plotted against our said Lord and the said Roman Church, anything to the hurt or prejudice of their persons, right, honor, state, or power; and if I shall know any such thing to be treated or agitated by any whatsoever, I will hinder it to the extent of my power, and, as soon as I can, will signify it to our said Lord, or to some other, by whom it may come to his knowledge. The rules of the holy fathers, the apostolic decrees, ordinances, or disposals, reservations, provisions, and mandates, I will observe with all my might, and cause to be observed by others. Heretics, schismatics, and rebels to our said Lord, or his aforesaid successors, I will, to the extent of my power, persecute and oppose."

THE OATH OF AN EPISCOPALIAN OR METHODIST MINISTER TO HIS PRESIDING ELDERS AND BISHOP.

"The bishop reads: 'And now that this present congregation of Christ here assembled may also understand your minds and wills in these things, and that *this your promise* may the more move you to do your duties, ye shall answer plainly to these things which we, IN THE NAME OF GOD and his Church, shall demand of you touching the same.'"

Is not this an *oath?* Is it not a solemn appeal to God? Is not this affirmation put in the name of God? It is then an oath.—(*See Webster's Dictionary.*)

The bishop then proceeds

"The Bishop: 'Will you REVERENTLY OBEY your *chief ministers,* unto whom is committed the *charge* and *government* over you; following with a glad mind and will *their* godly admonitions, submitting yourself to their GODLY JUDGMENTS?'

"Ans: 'I will do so, *the Lord being my helper!!'*"

Read it again—is it not a mistake? Can such a solemn, awful oath fall from a professing Christian's, much less Christian minister's lips? Read it:

"The Bishop says: 'Will you REVERENTLY OBEY *your chief ministers,* unto *whom* is committed the CHARGE AND GOVERNMENT OVER YOU; FOLLOWING WITH A GLAD MIND AND WILL THEIR GODLY ADMONITIONS, SUBMITTING YOURSELVES TO THEIR GODLY JUDGMENTS.'

"Answer of the elder: 'I will *so do,* the

Lord [forgive the poor deluded soul] being my helper!!'"

Blessed Savior! and can this be the language of one of *thy* ministers—of a Protestant Christian freeman, in the nineteenth century? And didst thou not most solemnly command thy disciples to acknowledge no master—no lawgiver, but thyself; and to teach only what thou hast enjoined upon them? And do they not here, as do the ministers of Antichrist, solemnly vow to take self-appointed lordlings for their masters, in all things, regardless of what thou hast commanded—and that so fully, so absolutely, as to exercise no judgment or will of their own in reserving any liberty to consult *thy will?*

Is not this a *more stringent oath* than the Catholic priests take to obey and do the bidding of their Pope? Does it not positively deprive one of the exercise of any mind, or will, or judgment of his own? Does it not reduce the Methodist circuit-rider and elder to a mere *passive tool*, blindly *subservient to the will and wishes* of their ghostly superiors? Am I mistaken? Read under the duties of preachers, Rule 12, which these Protestant ministers are especially asked if they have read and will observe:

"12th Rule. Act in all things, not according to *your own* will, but as a *son* (i. e. our servant) in the Gospel! As such it is your *duty* to employ your time in the manner which WE direct in preaching and visiting from house to house, in reading, meditation, and prayer. ABOVE ALL, [hear it, O ye heavens! and be astonished, O ye earth — hear it! above preaching the Gospel, reading God's Word, obeying Christ, or even prayer; yes, above *all*,] if you labor with us in the Lord's vineyard, it is needful that you should do that part of the work which WE advise, at those *times* and places which WE judge most for his glory!"

Slavery — spiritual serfdom — what shall we say? We have no language in which to express our feelings. Were an angel from heaven to presume to impose such a law upon a mortal, he would be thrust down to darkness in a moment; and for a mortal—a poor fallen mortal—to demand service of his fellow!

If this is not a bold example and illustration

of Antichrist, and the pretensions and blasphemous assumptions of the "Man of Sin," opposing and exalting himself above all that is called God, or that is worshiped; so that he, as God, sitteth in the temple of God, showing himself that he is God, the world has never yet beheld one!

Is not this an *antichristian* power, that makes implicit and *servile* obedience to its mandates the first and most important duty—the one above even the worship of God (prayer) and the reading or teaching his Word!—to heed and obey the will of man more than the will of God! This is setting man above God!

Can Baptists assail this principle of the Papacy without incurring the displeasure of every minister of the Episcopal and Methodist hierarchies?

8. *Will they charge the Catholics with blasphemy for giving the titles that belong to God to the pontiff, and cardinals, and bishops?*

Are not Episcopalians and Methodists guilty of the same sin? See the title given to the late Bishop Hedding, in the Methodist Preacher,

(Introduction, page 1 :) "THE RIGHT REVEREND FATHER IN GOD!" This smacks of my Lord God the Pope. See titles of the Episcopal clergy.

9. *Will they object to the Pope because he claims the power of the keys?*

The Protestant clergy claim *each* the same power! Methodist bishops and elders claim it, and Presbyterian ministers and their elders!

For a full discussion of this, see the Letter on "Key Power," page 247.

10. *Will Protestant sects attack the Catholics because they claim that the supreme visible headship is vested in the Pope of Rome, since the visible Church has no earthly head?*

But they have each a head! Queen Victoria and her parliament is the head of the Church of England, as Pio Nono and his bench of cardinals is of the Catholic; the bishops and General Conference is the head of the Methodist society, and the General Assembly of Presbyterianism — *all legislative bodies.* I should prefer one great, grand head to so many little heads!

11. *Will Protestants object to Popery on the ground of her traditions?*

They hold, teach, and practice her most pernicious one—that has done Christianity more injury than all the other traditions of Popery together! Infant baptism is a *tradition* of "the Church," as well as *sprinkling* and *pouring upon* for baptism, and Catholics have never failed to cast it into the teeth of Protestants, that while they protest against the authority of the Romish Church, they practice one of her principal traditions.

What says Dr. Pise, (a priest of the Romish Church, and of high standing among that order in New York, second, perhaps, to none but Bishop Hughes,) in a lecture recently delivered in New York: "There are many things believed by all Christians at the present day, not to be found in the Scriptures. This is true with regard to infant baptism, that we and all Christians (Pedobaptist) believe in, for there is no authority for it in Scripture. We nowhere find that the apostles baptized infants, and if it be proper and necessary to baptize infants as well as adults, we have no other authority, and MUST DEPEND ENTIRELY ON TRADITION"—of the Church of Rome, of course.

I add to this the highest Roman Catholic authority in the world, that of Mons. Bossuet, Bishop of Meaux, who was preceptor to one of the kings of France, and the frank concession to that authority by the learned Mons. de la Roque, pastor of a Reformed Church at Rouen, in Normandy, who was engaged in controversy with Bishop Bossuet. Bossuet says:

"In fine, we read not in the Scripture that baptism was otherwise administered, [than by immersion;] and we are able to make it appear by the acts of councils, and by the ancient rituals, that for thirteen hundred years baptism was thus administered throughout the whole Church, as far as was possible.

"Though these are incontestable truths, yet neither we [Catholics] nor those of the pretended Reformed religion hearken to the Anabaptists, who hold mersion to be essential and indispensable; nor have either they [Protestants] or we [Catholics] feared to change this dipping (as I may say) of the whole body, into a bare aspersion or infusion on one part of it. No other reason of this alteration can be rendered than that this dipping is not of the substance of baptism; and those of the pretended Reformed religion agreeing with us in this, the first principle we have laid down is incontestable."

And in another place:

"Jesus Christ (says he) has ordered to *dip*, as we have often observed. We have also taken notice, that he was baptized in this form, that his apostles practiced it, and that it was continued in the Church down to the twelfth and thirteenth ages; and yet baptism given only by infusion [sprinkling or pouring] is admitted, without any difficulty, on the sole authority of the Church."

"Experience has shown that all the attempts of the Reformed to confound the Anabaptists by the Scripture, have been weak; and therefore they are at last obliged to allege to them the practice of the Church. We see in their Discipline, at the end of the eleventh chapter, the form of receiving adult persons into their communion, where they make the proselyted Anabaptist acknowledge that the baptism of infants *is founded on Scripture and on the perpetual practice of the Church!* When the pretended Reformed believe they have the word of God very expressly on their side, they are not wont to build on the perpetual practice of the Church. But in this case, because the Scripture furnishes them with nothing by which they are able to stop the mouths of the Anabaptists, it was necessary to rely on somewhat else, and at the same time to confess that in these matters the perpetual practice of the Church is of inviolable authority."

What reply did the Reformed pastor make to this authority? Did he deny that Christ commanded his disciples to immerse, and not to sprinkle? Did he deny that it had been the practice of thirteen centuries? Did he deny that the Romish Church had, upon her sole authority, changed the action into sprinkling? No; he denies not one of the above statements, but frankly admits every one of them, and charges the Romish Church with having corrupted the ordinances by so doing.

He repeats at length what the bishop urges against the Protestants concerning the change of *dipping* into *sprinkling*, etc., in which they agree with those of the Romish Church, and then answers in the following terms:

"I was willing (says he) to report the whole passage of Mons. Bossuet, to elucidate this matter to the Protestants, who scarce ever make any reflection on it. It is true that the greatest part of them hithorto baptize only by *sprinkling*, but it is certainly an *abuse;* and this practice, which they have retained from the Romish Church without a due examination of it, as well as many other things which they still retain, renders their baptism very defective. It corrupts both the institution and ancient usage of it, and the relation it ought to have to faith, repentance, and regeneration. Mons. Bossuet's remark, that *dipping* was in use for thirteen hundred years, deserves our serious consideration, and our acknowledgment thereupon, that we have not sufficiently examined *all that we have retained from the Romish Church;* that seeing her most learned prelates now inform us that it was *she* that first abolished a usage authorized by so many strong reasons, and by so many ages, she has done very ill on this occasion, and that we are obliged to return to the ancient practice of the Church, and to the institution of Jesus Christ. I do not say that baptism by aspersion is null—that is not my opinion; but it must be confessed, if sprinkling destroys not the substance of baptism, yet it alters it, and in some sort corrupts it—it is a defect which spoils its lawful form."—*Stennet's Answer to Russen,* p. 186.

I have quoted this to give a practical illustration of how utterly impossible it is for Pedobaptists to meet the Papists. The old mother has every conceivable advantage.

12. *Will they denounce Popery for its opposition to the circulation of the pure word of God, so that every man may have every word of the " Word of Life" faithfully translated into his own language?*

Protestants, as sects, are bitterly opposed to the purest possible version in all languages and tongues, and, indeed, to-day, are giving a *pure version to no nation of earth!* Did they not refuse to circulate the version made by Dr. Judson, because it translated every word?

13. *Is not Popery an absolute and tyrannical hierarchy, oppressive to humanity, hostile to its best interests, and, in its influence, opposed to, and destructive of, all free institutions, as of civil and religious liberty?*

It is manifest to all that the leading Protestant sects are hierarchies, or despotic aristocracies also, since the people are denied all voice in the administration of government, and the authority, legislative and executive, is placed in the hands of a few. It is a fixed fact, and easy of *clearest demonstration*, that *hierarchial* and *aristocratic* Church organizations are hostile in their influence to republican institutions; that they insensibly prepare the rising generation to favor, if not to seek, a civil government of the *same character*. It is admitted that nothing is more dangerous than a religious hierarchy or monarchy in a republic. Is the Roman hierarchy dangerous, and are the *Protestant* hierarchies less so? It is the *principle*, not the *name;* for a hierarchy is subversive of religious freedom, in whose hands soever it may be.

Lutheranism in the hands of Luther was opposed to civil and religious liberty, and he united his "Church" to the State in adulterous union, and it has been from then until now a persecuting power. Presbyterianism in the hands of Calvin burned Servetus in a slow fire of green wood, and drove, by fines, imprisonments, and tortures, the Baptists from the Canton of Geneva.

Episcopalianism is black and bloody with the murders of the martyrs of Jesus. Smithfield will witness against her in the judgment of nations that will come. (See Matt. xxiv.) Puritanism and Presbyterianism in New England, and the Episcopacy in Virginia and Georgia made manifest their opposition to religious freedom, in the bloody acts they committed in their mad attempts to crush it out, and prevent its gaining a foothold on these shores. All these are to-day opposed to free religious discussion by the pulpit and the press.

The time is not far distant when Protestant hierarchies will be repudiated by all Christians, as the Papal is to-day.

14. *Will Protestants charge upon Catholics that they recognize and support the adulterous union of Church and State, telling them that the Church of Christ " is not of this world ?"*

Rome could reply: " You, my daughters, have committed *harlotry* and made yourselves the ' abominations of the earth ' by the same act.

Where have you had the power, and have not united the State to your Churches? Have not Episcopalians done so in England, and all her colonies, and did they not retain the union in America so long as possible? Have not the Presbyterians in Scotland, and in all the continental kingdoms of Europe, as well as Lutherans, and did they not do the same thing in the American colonies?"

15. *Will Protestants denounce Rome because she denies the supremacy of the Word of God, placing as she does, the decisions of her councils and of her pontiffs before it, for the observance of her people?*

Can not Rome point the Episcopalians to their head—the reigning king, or even woman, and the Parliament of England, Presbyterians to their General Assemblies, and Methodists to their College of Bishops and General Conferences, to whose decisions they are all compelled to bow implicitly or be excommunicated?

16. *Will Protestants charge the Papacy with denying that doctrine professedly so sacred to Pedobaptists*—THE ALL-SUFFICIENCY *of the Word*

of God for faith and practice?—the Bible and the Bible alone, for all religious doctrines and duties?

Can not Rome point to their Books of Common Prayer, Rubrics, etc., Confession of Faith, and authenticated Disciplines, that in every Protestant meeting-house are placed either on top of the Bible or by its side, but in every case the first required to be observed by Protestants. If the laws, and traditions, and "rules" enjoined by their elders and "chief ministers" on them are not observed, the guilty protestant is cast out of the Church of Christ—if these organizations can be so considered. Does Rome do worse?

17. *Will Protestants assail the Papacy for sweeping away the great fundamental vital doctrine of individualism, upon which all true Christianity rests, because she forbids by pains and penalties personal religious liberty, and freedom of the conscience, and forces upon her infantile, unconscious subjects, onerous rites, Church ordinances, and religious obligations, and even salvation, without either faith or voluntariness on their part.*

Would not Rome reply: " Whenever you judge me on this you condemn yourselves. You have imitated my example and adopted the very rite which I originated, by which to accomplish these very results, that I might the more easily and successfully extend my authority over the hearts and consciences of men. Were it now in your power as it has been, to carry out your principles, you would not only as thoroughly destroy the pure doctrine of personal religion, but constrain religious freedom and liberty of conscience, by 'pains and penalties,' as you have done. But you are more inconsistent than I am. While you teach the doctrine of total hereditary depravity in your Creed, you deny it in your Ritual, (for the baptism of infants,) and while you deny in your Creed the possibility of the apostasy from grace of a saint or the elect, you deny it in your Discipline." I give Rome the advantage of an extract from an able review of New England Puritanism : *

"And we can not refuse to see that as per-

---

* Christian Review, No. 66.

secution was a settled element of their policy, so it was the natural outgrowth of their principles. Infant baptism is in its very idea opposed to individualism. It nips religious liberty in the very bud. It blasts it in the very germ. It extirpates it at the very root. It begins by instituting sponsors for the faith of the child. It anticipates his birth, and by some mysterious process marries on the spiritual life of the child to the spiritual life of his progenitors. It does not leave him the poor privilege of being born in original sin. If, with the pious old lady, he should ever come to the conclusion that if he lost his total depravity, he would lose all his religion, his case would be hopeless. He can neither believe nor disbelieve for himself. When he grows up to moral consciousness and the period of moral responsibility, he finds, by some spiritual legerdemain, by some mysterious law of hereditary transmission, that responsibility shifted to another, and a corresponding disposition of his outward relations. While yet unborn, linked with his believing parent, he was safely infolded in the bosom of the covenant, and as soon as born has been snugly sheltered in the bosom of the Church. In unconscious infancy the vows of the Church have been laid upon him; the sacred obligations of the Christian profession assumed in his behalf. He can not quit the Church to which he has been attached in infancy, or remain aloof from it, without a forcible sundering of bands which have been cast around him. He can not think for himself without being liable to be dealt with for heresy. He can not act for himself without being liable to be dealt with for contumacy. The Church has thrown her arms around him and she claims him as her own. 'That children, by baptism,' so runs the Westminster Declaration, approved by the General Assembly of Scotland, 'are solemnly received into the bosom of the visible Church, distinguished from the world, and them that are without, and united with believers; and that all who are baptized in the name of Christ do renounce, and by their baptism are bound to fight against the devil, the world, and the flesh; that they are Christians and federally holy before baptism, and therefore, they are baptized; that the inward grace and virtue of baptism is not tied to that very moment of time wherein it is administered, and that the fruit and power thereof reacheth to the whole course of our life.' Ah, could the ordinance but realize these professions made in its behalf! Could the holy water sprinkled on the brow, and the holy name uttered over it, really prove the talisman which it claims to be against the baleful workings of the great Foe— the enemy more potent and terrible than Death! But

"'Alas! Leviathan is not so tamed,'

and he mocks at the impotent weapon which recoils from his dragon-scales.

"Now that the principle of voluntariness in religion is thus cut up at the root, that for it the principle of coercion is substituted, is self-evident. The man is bound to the Church by obligations laid upon him when he was yet unconscious, and knew neither good nor evil. And the Church having begun her work must finish it. Him whom she has brought under her discipline she must subject to her discipline; and as many may be disposed to break away and ignore the authority thus assumed over them, she must look around for some means of enforcing her claims. Her natural, her only appeal is to the arm of the civil magistrate, and her first business is, therefore, to put herself in alliance with the State.

"And here another principle comes in to her aid. The doctrine is that the child of the believer is born a Christian, and that because he is a Christian he is baptized and is a genuine member of the Church. Assume now that this is no idle parade of words, but a doctrine honestly believed and acted upon. The inevitable consequence follows. Once a Christian always a Christian, is true both for himself and his descendants ' to the last syllable of recorded time.' Piety and Church membership both become hereditary, and spread themselves by fixed and certain laws through all the ramifications, and to every individual, of the race of the godly. By necessary consequence, then, individual Christianity is lost in family Christianity, and the religion of the family soon merges into the religion of the State. Why should it not? Church and State become coincident in territory and population. The members of the State are all members of the Church, and it may well behoove them to devolve on some one, and on whom more appropriately than on the civil magistrate, the charge of seeing that none are derelict in duty; that no child is allowed, through the remissness of his parents, to lose the benefits of a rite whose consequences are so momentous, nor when grown up, to shake off the yoke of obligation which the watchful benevolence of the Church has placed upon his infant neck.

"Such, logically, such in fact, was New England Congregationalism. It broke off from a national Church which it did not like, to come over the seas and found a national Church which it did like. On the soil on which it had set its foot it planted the banner of unlimited dominion. Its parishes were territorial parishes. Its Churches were territorial Churches. It claimed the fealty of every soul born within its limits. The civil magistrate was but the instrument of the spiritual power, and dissent from the recognized modes of worship was punished as alike disobedience to God and rebellion against the State.

"Just as little is it accidental that Baptists have been the uniform advocates of religious freedom, and that single-handed they have fought the battle against the banded sentiment of Christendom. It flows necessarily from their first principle. Their doctrine of individualism—of personal faith and voluntary baptism—draws along with it as with the sweep of a cataract, the absolute repudiation of all State interference between the conscience and its God. The claim of the civil power to coerce men into religious faith and union with the Church, becomes a grand impertinence—only not utterly ridiculous, because audaciously wicked. To his own master each one standeth or falleth. He is in immediate, untransferable, inviolable relations to God, and neither man nor angel can wrest from him the privilege, nor lift from him the obligation of his high spiritual prerogative. By a logical necessity, therefore—by every principle and the whole spirit of his system, every Baptist is committed to the advocacy of religious liberty. And by a necessity equally strong, every *consistent* Pedobaptist is committed against it [as fully as the Papist.] Innocent as infant baptism seems, as slight a thing as it appears to lay the consecrating hand on the brow of the unconscious babe, and utter over it the sacred formula, it is in fact a thing of wondrous potency. If it has not precisely the consequences which the Confession assigns to it, it has others scarcely less far-reaching, and of less questionable reality. Its tendency is to invite the world into the arms of the Church and then to throttle the Church in the embrace of the world. It has thus linked itself with spiritual despotism, and is at this moment in Europe the strong bond of alliance between the Church and the State.

"Nor can we fail to remark how utterly discordant is the doctrine on which infant baptism rests, with the spirit of Calvinism. An especial characteristic of the system of Calvin is its assertion of original depravity, and of our absolute dependence for moral purity on regenerating grace. How these two doctrines--an absolute heirdom of wrath, and inherited Church membership—can 'dwell together in unity,' it is impossible to discover. They are irreconcilably hostile. Like two distinct races dwelling together on the same soil, one must hold its ground at the expense of the other. In New England's early history the hereditary principle prevailed. Religion, therefore, rapidly declined from its purity. The Church was inundated by the world—by men who had no sympathy with its vital doctrines; to whom the cross was a stumbling-block, and evangelical religion foolishness. Hence, the Church lay cold and dead in the arms of her baptized enemies, until the Great Revival awoke her slumbering life. Since then, in that portion of the Church which did not renounce evangelical doctrines and faith, the Calvinistic element has been in the ascendant, and infant baptism has shrunk into little more than a ceremony, a form of dedication by which the parent seeks to deepen his own sense of responsibility, and secure he knows not what spiritual benefit to his offspring."

I could continue this list of principles, in common with Protestants and Papists, to double the number, were it necessary; but these are sufficient for my purpose, to show that the Reformation must be radically *reformed*, and Protestantism *itself protested* against, before it can successfully grapple with the Papacy, or deserve to receive the countenance of republican-loving American Christians.

We also see the unfortunate antagonism with all the Protestant sects, into which we, as Baptists, are brought whenever we attack the *principles* of the Papacy! Our blows break their force upon Protestants; and Catholic priests smile in security behind them, as behind a bulwark. We can only reach Romanists through Protestants, for they are intrenched behind them. Their priests the more securely keep them in darkness by directing their attention to the fact that Protestants hold and practice their traditions, and defend *nearly all their important principles!* It requires great moral courage and Christian heroism in Baptists to attack these principles, since they know they will be precipitated into a fierce conflict with all Protestant sects, and expose themselves to their displeasure, hatred, and often their bitter persecutions.

This ought not so to be. We can not believe that the Savior ever intended *his* followers to be thus divided and conflicting. We believe there are many precious Christians in the Pedobaptist sects, *though in great error.* We have no bitterness—nothing but love in our heart toward them, and this leads us to pray for them, and endeavor to convince them of their error; to leave men and follow Christ. They should unite with *us* against the in-rolling flood of Catholicism, if they love their country or the religion of Christ: and they can not do this so long as they hold the distinctive principles of the *Papacy* in common with Papists. We beseech them for the sake of their land and religion, to repudiate these and unite with us upon the word of God, and let the *Bible and the Bible alone, be our religion.* Let our principles be blazoned upon our banner:

A PURE BIBLE ONLY—OUR PRAYER-BOOK, CONFESSION, AND DISCIPLINE.

NO REGENERATION BUT THE HOLY SPIRIT AND THE WORD OF GOD.

NO SALVATION BUT BY GRACE. OBSERVING

ALL THINGS, AND THOSE ONLY, WHICH CHRIST COMMANDED, AND AS HE COMMANDED.

I protest I have not noticed the Papal features of Protestantism but with the kindest feelings and the purest motives. These are the *weak points of Protestantism.* It is behind the age, as well as unsupported by the Bible. The Reformation needs another Luther. Were he once more to direct it, we have reason to believe that, with the light of this age, he would reform it of every feature of Romanism; he would effect the reformation he so ardently desired in his day, restore to it the primitive immersion of believers, and republicanize its government. Protestantism was chilled in the *shadow* of the sixteenth century. It has made no advancement. It is still either afraid to trust the people with self-government, or its clergy have become too corrupt to yield up the reins and scepter of ecclesiastical domination. The nineteenth century has demonstrated the truth of God's word, that man is capable of, and created for self-government, and that it is the only form of government that will secure for humanity, individually or nationally, in Church or State, the proper incentive to progress, the largest freedom, and the greatest happiness. Let Protestantism, then, bow to this fact, and grant to its membership the inalienable right which the Creator and Redeemer of man vouchsafed him, and which the Papal and Protestant clergy have so long and so iniquitously usurped and withheld from him.

CHAPTER V.

THE CLAIMS OF BAPTISTS.

Did Baptists spring from the Papal Church, or receive their Ordinations and Baptisms from the Man of Sin ?

BAPTISTS claim that they are successors to the "Witnesses of Jesus," who preserved the faith *once* delivered to the saints, and kept the ordinances as they were originally committed to the primitive Churches. They claim to be the lineal descendants of the martyrs who, for so many ages, sealed their testimony with their blood. They claim that they can trace the history of communities, essentially like themselves, back through the "wilderness," into which they were driven by the dragon, and the beast that succeeded to him, and the image of the beast, by *a trail of blood*, lighted up by a thousand stake-fires, until that blood mingles with the blood of the apostles, and the Son of God, and John the Baptist. They believe that they never did, ecclesiastically, symbolize with the Papacy, but ever repudiated it as Antichrist, and withdrew from it, and refused to recognize its baptisms or ordinances, or its priests as the ministers of Christ. These are bold claims, we admit; yet, if we can sustain them successfully against those of any other communion, it is not only our *right*, but our imperative *duty* to do so.

I propose to do so, not by Baptist testimony, but by the united and concurrent testimony of Protestants and Papists.

It would be conceded by any judge or jury that my case was an incontestable one, should I sustain it, beyond a doubt, *by the witnesses of my opponent!*

1. *It has been charged that American Baptists sprang from Roger Williams, and their baptisms from his informal and unscriptural one.*

The facts are, that Roger Williams never was a *member*, much less a *minister*, of any Baptist Church in England or America. He was converted to, and advocated, their views of baptism and civil and religious liberty. It is true that he immersed Ezekiel Holliman, who, in turn, baptized him; and he again, ten or eleven others; and so formed a society; but he continued with it only four months, when he repudiated what he had done, and his society soon came to nothing. Cotton Mather, the cotemporary of Williams, a distinguished Pedobaptist Puritan minister, (see Mather's History,) said it soon came to nothing.

It can not be shown that any Baptist Church sprang from Williams's affair.

Nor can it be proved that the baptism of any Baptist minister came from Williams's hands.

The oldest Baptist Church in America is the one now existing, with her original articles of faith, in Newport, R. I., and she was planted by Dr. John Clark before Williams was baptized. He received his baptism in Elder Stillwell's Church in London, and that Church received hers from the Dutch Baptists of Holland, sending over a minister to be baptized by them. These Baptists descended from the Waldenses, whose historical line reaches far back and connects with the Donatists, and theirs to the Apostolical Churches.

A writer in the *Christian Review* condenses the facts of history* into the following eleven statements, which can be confidently relied upon:

"1. Roger Williams was baptized by Ezekiel Holliman, March, 1639, and immediately after, he baptized Mr. Holliman and ten others.

"2. These formed a Church, or Society, of which Roger Williams was the pastor.

"Four months after his baptism, that is, in July following, W. left the Church, and never afterward returned to it. As his doubts respecting baptism and the perpetuity of the Church, which led to this step, must have commenced soon after his baptism, it is not likely that he baptized any others.

"4. The Church which Williams formed, 'came to nothing,' or was dissolved soon after he left it.

"5. It was reorganized, or another was

---

* If any one wishes to see the documents themselves, let him send for a little work entitled "*The First Baptist Church in Providence not the First Baptist Church in America*," 25 cts.

formed a few days afterward, under Mr. Thomas Olney as its pastor, who was one of the eleven baptized by Roger Williams. Olney continued to be the pastor of this Church until his death, in 1682, somewhat over 30 years.

"6. In 1653 or '54, which was a few years after the formation of Olney's Church, there was a division in that Church on the question of 'laying on of hands" in the reception of members, and a separate Church was formed for the maintenance of this ceremony, under the pastorship of Chad Browne, Wickenden, and Dexter. This Church was perpetuated, having, in 1808, given up its original faith as to the laying on of hands, and is now the First Baptist Church in Providence.

"7. The parent Church, under Olney, gradually dwindled away, and became extinct about the year 1718, some seventy years from its origin.

"8. No Church was formed from Olney's after the division already mentioned, and no ministers are known to have gone out from it. Olney's baptism, whether valid or invalid, was not propagated.

"9. Nearly a century passed before the Church formed from Olney's began to colonize, in 1730.

"10. None of its ministers, or the ministers of the Churches formed from it, received their baptism from Williams, or from any one whose baptisms descended from his.

"11. The Baptist Churches of America, then, could not have descended from Roger Williams, or from the temporary society which he formed. Their true descent is from the Baptist Churches of Wales and Piedmont, extending back to the apostles' times."

2. *It has been charged that Baptists are the descendants of the fanatical Anabaptists of Munster.*

But few now are so reckless as to make this charge, since it has been so clearly refuted by Baptists and admitted by so many candid Pedobaptist scholars. Only a certain class of Pedobaptists, *the basest sort* of their ministry, propagate this slander now. Merle D'Aubigné, a Presbyterian, and the distinguished author of the History of the Reformation, who had a perfect acquaintance with all the facts, and wrote upon the very ground, in the preface to his work published by the American Tract Society, says:

"On one point, it seems necessary to guard against misapprehension. Some persons imagine that the Anabaptists of the times of the Reformation, and the Baptists of our day, are the same. But they are as different as possible."

Fessenden's *Encyclopedia* (quoted with approbation by D'Aubigné) says:

"ANABAPTIST.—The English and Dutch Baptists do not consider the word as at all applicable to their sect. It is but justice to observe that the Baptists of Holland, England, and the United States, are essentially distinct from those seditious and fanatical individuals above mentioned; as they profess an equal aversion to all principles of rebellion of the one, and enthusiasm of the other.—*Preface to Reformation, p.* 10.

The fact is, the Munster Anabaptists were many of them *sprinklers*, who were dissidents from Rome but not converts to the Lutheran or Genevan creeds, and therefore, equally obnoxious to the displeasure of Luther and Calvin. A writer has well said:

"Under the very *generic* name of Anabaptist, the greatest imaginable variety of characters passed—that some were 'sober and virtuous' persons, while many others were mere 'political speculators and adventurers.'"

Now it is an act of the greatest injustice to call all these Baptists. Are we to be stigmatized for the doings of *sprinklers?* or to be blamed with the faults of infant baptizers? or to be held accountable for the misdemeanors of "mere political speculators and adventurers?" We never acknowledged any such thing in our Zion. They are *anti*-Baptists. Those Anabaptists who were of "the genuine Baptist order," disclaimed all connections with the political religious mass. We must separate between those who were truly and properly Baptists, or as their enemies term them, *Anabaptists*, and all that impure and gross religious material, which is received as theirs by unfair and designing Pedobaptist historians. The Reformation deluged the Baptist Zion with hundreds and thousands who were scarcely cleansed from the polluting embraces of the mother of harlots. They were dragged from the cloisters, and convents, and confessionals of mystical Babylon by the magic names of Luther and Calvin; but they were only half awakened. Their notions were crude and ill-digested, and ready to be guided by any and every master spirit; and if, forsooth, they did not in every particular, subscribe the *Lutheran* or *Zwinglian* creeds, whether of Church or State, they were straightway styled *Anabaptists*. Hence, we find almost all kinds of persons bearing this title. But a "portion of them were of the genuine Baptist order;" this was a little nucleus of *true saints*, around whose Zion both Protestants and Catholics "heaped their cast-off rubbish, as if the more easily to consume it with their fiery persecutions." But the genuine Anabaptists existed to repudiate the very first appearance and workings of the "Man of Sin." Before Luther protested, or the Papacy was, they are. They existed as a distinct people ages before these Protestant daughters of Rome were born. They were the only "salt of the earth," and the "light of the world," during the sixteen hundred years that preceded the Reformation. The Baptists alone supplied that host of martyrs, whose souls John saw under the throne, impatient for their names and testimony to be vindicated by the coming of the Son of God.

I bring forward here Mosheim, one of their bitterest enemies, a distinguished *Lutheran* historian, whose work is universally a standard. He so hated the faith of the Baptists, as to stigmatize it as " a *flagitious and intolerable heresy.*" Yet this historian, while he could trace each existing Protestant and Papist sect back to the very *day* of its birth, and to the *spot* of its origin, and give the name of its *father and founder*, and give us *every year* of its history—showing that no *wilderness-like obscurity*, no hiding, could be predicated of them—yet he was forced to admit that the origin of the Baptists was of no modern date, but *hidden in the remote depths of antiquity:*

"The true origin of that sect which acquired the name of Anabaptists, by their administering anew the rite of baptism to those who came over to their communion, and derived that of Mennonites from that famous man to whom they owe the greatest part of their *present* felicity, IS HID IN THE REMOTE DEPTHS OF ANTIQUITY, and is, consequently, extremely difficult to be ascertained."—*Vol. iv, pp.* 427, 8, *Maclaine's Edition of* 1811.

Again:

"It may be observed that the Mennonites are not entirely mistaken when they boast of their descent from the Waldenses, Petrobrussians, and other *ancient sects*, who were usually considered as witnesses of the truth, in the times of universal darkness and superstition. Before the rise of Luther and Calvin, there lay, *concealed* [this looks like a fulfillment of the Revelation, where we find the woman driven into the wilderness— *i. e.*, obscurity!] in almost all the countries of Europe, particularly in Bohemia, Moravia, Switzerland, and Germany, many persons who adhered tenaciously to the following doctrines, which the Waldenses, Wicliffites and Hussites, [we do not feel reproached by association with such spirits,] had maintained, some in a more disguised, and others in a more public manner. viz.: "That the kingdom of Christ, or the visible Church he had established upon earth, was an assembly of true and real saints, and ought, therefore, to be inaccessible to the wicked and unrighteous, and also exempt from all those institutions which human prudence suggests, to oppose the progress of iniquity, or to correct and reform transgressors."

This is a frank admission that the Waldenses, as well as the Wicliffites, were opposed to *infant* baptism and Church membership, since they admitted none but "*real saints,*" into the visible Church, and that they—as Baptists have ever been—were opposed to a religion of *force and persecution.*

We would be willing to rest the claims of Baptists to the highest antiquity, and to Scriptural orthodoxy, upon this testimony alone.

Now, let a Presbyterian testify concerning the antiquity of Baptists. We ask Zwingle, the celebrated Swiss reformer, who was cotemporary with Luther, Munzer, and Stork:

"The institution of Anabaptism is no novelty, but for thirteen hundred years has caused great disturbance in the Church, and has acquired such a strength, that the attempt in this age to contend with it, appeared futile for a time."

DEATH BY THREE HORNS. 131

This carries our history back to A. D. 225! Zwingle, may well say that Anabaptism had acquired great strength in his day.

In the little State of Bohemia alone, Baptists numbered eighty thousand.

One of the Waldensian bards, George Morell, stated that in his day, 1533, there were more than eight hundred thousand persons professing the faith of the Waldenses.*

Lemborch, professor of divinity in the University of Amsterdam, and who wrote a history of the Inquisition, in comparing the Waldenses with the Christians of his own times, says:

"To speak honestly what I think of all the modern sects of Christians, the Dutch Baptists most resemble both the Albigenses and Waldenses, but particularly the latter."†

But, have we not been persecuted and worn down for, lo! these twelve hundred years? Has not the Apocalyptic "WOMAN," during all this

---

* See Orchard, vol. 1, page 286.
† Robinson's Ecclesiastical Researches, p. 311.

time, been drunk with our blood, and heaven filling with our martyred brethren?

We appeal to Cardinal Hosius, President of the Council of Trent, (A. D. 1650,) the most learned and powerful Catholic of his day. Hear him testify:

"If the truth of religion were to be judged of by the readiness and cheerfulness which a man of any sect shows in suffering, then the opinion and persuasion of no sect can be *truer* and *surer* than that of Anabaptists, [Baptists,] since there have been *none, for these twelve hundred years past, that have been more generally punished*, or that have more cheerfully and steadfastly undergone, and even offered themselves to, *the most cruel sorts* of punishment, than these people."

"The Anabaptists are a pernicious sect, of which kind the Waldensian brethren seem also to have been. Nor is this heresy a modern thing, for it existed in the time of Austin."—*Rees's Reply to Wall, p.* 20.

Austin was born A. D. 354. This gives Baptists a high antiquity; and the fact that Austin was not baptized in infancy, and yet was born of

Christian parents, proves that Pedobaptism was not in existence, or, at least, not very general, in this century. That infant baptism was a *new thing* in this early age, is proved by the additional facts that neither Basil, Bishop of Nicene, nor Chrysostom, nor Jerome of Strydon, nor Theodore, the Emperor, nor Gregory Nazienzen, nor Ambrose, nor Polycrates, nor Nectaries, nor Constantine the Great, were baptized in infancy, though born of Christian parents.*

We add the following from Orchard, vol. i, p. 49:

"Dr. Field observes, on the histories of these great men,† 'that very many that were born of Christian parents, in the fourth and fifth centuries, delayed their baptism for a long time, insomuch that many were made bishops before they were baptized.' The same views are sup-

---

* See *Robinson's History of Baptism*, chap. xiii, sec. 5, and *Wall*, vol. iv.

† Since these names, with others which could be recorded, are some of the most distinguished for respectability, in the annals of history, *one plain evidence* enforces itself upon our attention, that *Pedobaptism* was unknown among royalty, courtiers, and respectable persons in Europe, at the period of these eminent men's births.

ported by Beatus Rhenanus, and Mr. Den; the latter mentions Pancratius, Pontius, Nazarius, Tecla, Luigerus, Erasma Tusca, all offsprings of believers, and yet not baptized till aged. Similar observations are made by the learned Daille and Dr. Barlow.*

" The great champion for infant baptism, Dr. W. Wall, remarks: 'It seems to me that the instances which the Baptists give of persons not baptized in infancy, though born of Christian parents, are not, if the matter of fact be true, so inconsiderable as this last plea [the sayings of the Fathers] would represent. On the contrary, *the persons they mention are* SO MANY, *and* SUCH NOTED PERSONS, that, if they be allowed, it is an argument that leaving children unbaptized was no unusual, but a frequent and ordinary thing; for, it is obvious to conclude, that if we can, in so remote an age, trace the practice of *so many* that did this, it is probable that a *great many more* of whose birth and baptism we do not read *did the like*. This I will own, that it seems to me the argument of the greatest weight of any that is brought on the Baptist side in this dispute about antiquity.' "†

---

* Danver's Treat., p. 72. Daille's Use of the Fathers, b. 2, ch. 6, Reas. 6, p. 149.

† History of Inf. Bap., p. 2, § 16, p. 42. We admit

We conclude this chapter with the words of Curcelleus:

"Pedobaptism was not known in the world the two first ages after Christ; in the third and fourth it was approved *by few;* at length in the fifth and following ages, it began to obtain in divers places; and therefore, we (Pedobaptists) observe this rite, indeed, as an ancient custom, but not as an apostolic tradition. The custom of baptizing infants did not begin before the third age after Christ, and that there appears not the least footstep of it for the first two centuries."*

But we have yet the crowning testimony of two Pedobaptist historians, that should convince the most incredulous of our candid opponents.

In the year 1819, Dr. Ypeij, Professor of the University of Gunningen, and Dr. J. J. Dermout, chaplain to the King of Holland, distinguished Pedobaptist scholars, published a history, in four volumes, entitled, "*History of the Reformed Church of the Netherlands*"—of which

---

sprinkling to be more ancient than John, Jesus, or Moses. (See Robinson's Hist. of Bap. c. 6, pp. 39–42.)

* Stennett's Ans., etc., p. 87.

Church they were members—in which work they devote a chapter to the history of the Dutch Baptists. I have space for only the frank statement of the conclusion to which their impartial investigation led them:

"We have now seen that the Baptists, who were formerly called Anabaptists, and in later times Mennonites, were the original Waldenses, and who have long, in the history of the Church, received the honor of that origin. ON THIS ACCOUNT, THE BAPTISTS MAY BE CONSIDERED THE ONLY CHRISTIAN COMMUNITY WHICH HAS STOOD SINCE THE APOSTLES, AND AS A CHRISTIAN SOCIETY WHICH HAS PRESERVED PURE THE DOCTRINE OF THE GOSPEL THROUGH ALL AGES. The perfectly correct external economy of the Baptist denomination, tends to confirm the truth disputed by the Romish Church, that the Reformation brought about in the sixteenth century was in the highest degree necessary; and at the same time goes to refute the erroneous notions of the Catholics, that their communion is the most ancient."—See *Encyclopedia of Religious Knowledge*, Art. MENNONITES; also, the *Southern Baptist Review*, Vol. v, No. 1, Art. 1, for full translation of the chapter.

That Dermout and Ypeij are not unsupported by historical authority, in their statements respecting the difference between the Anabaptists and the Baptists, will appear from an article in "The New Royal Encyclopedia." This great work, by Wm. H. Hall, Esq., with other learned, ingenious gentlemen, was begun in London in 1788, and completed in three large folio volumes. In the article "Anabaptists," after recounting the excesses of Muntzer, Matthias, Borkholdt, and others, during the sixteenth century, in Germany, the Encyclopedia proceeds:

"It is to be remarked that the Baptists or Mennonites in England and Holland are to be considered in a very different light from the enthusiasts we have been describing, and it appears equally uncandid and invidious to trace up their distinguished sentiments, as some of their adversaries have done, to those obnoxious characters, and then to stop, in order, as it were, to associate with it the ideas of turbulence and fanaticism, with which it certainly has no natural connection. Their coincidence with some of those oppressed and infatuated people in denying baptism to infants, is acknowledged by the Baptists, but they disavow the practice which the appellation of Anabaptists implies; and their doctrines seem referable to a more ancient and respectable origin. They appear supported by history in considering themselves the descendants of the Waldenses, who were so grievously oppressed and persecuted by the despotic heads of the Romish hierarchy."

We have thus indicated, but by no means exhausted, our sources of proof, in establishing the claims of the Baptist denomination to be the community established by Christ as his visible Church. The Welsh Baptists trace their unbroken descent from apostolic times; and from Wales came many of our earliest Churches in America.*

Baptists not only can lay a just claim to the highest antiquity of any acknowledged Christian community, but to them belongs the distinguishing honor of having been the first, and for nearly eighteen centuries the only, assertors of civil

---

* Those who wish to be satisfied with the strength of our claims will do well to read, after the New Testament, Orchard's Chronological History of the Baptists, vols. i. and ii.; *Robinson's History of Baptism, and Ecclesiastical Researches*, vols. i. and ii.

and religious liberty. In whatever land the inestimable right is to-day enjoyed, it was planted there by Baptist hands, and watered by Baptist blood. Not only against the Popes of Rome, but against the Reformers, Luther, Zwingle, and Calvin, did the Baptists maintain this doctrine.

Not to Luther, or his Church, does the world attribute the principle, *that the conscience of no one should be constrained or coerced in religious matters;* for, as an opposer and persecutor of the Anabaptists, he had no equal in his day—stirring up the princes of Germany to annihilate them from their dominions, as he did by his letters, and prodigious numbers were devoted to death in its most dreadful forms.*

Not to Zwingle, the Swiss Presbyterian, who instigated the cantons of Switzerland to pass such murderous laws, which devoted to cruel death so many Baptist men and women; not to Zwingle, who pronounced the death sentence, and its form, upon the noble Hubmeyer, "his old friend, the companion of his earlier studies,"

---

* Mosheim, vol. iii, p. 79.

who, in the sacred relations of friend and fellow-student, had known his doubts on baptism, and had himself felt their force. This man, the father of Swiss Presbyterianism, "is reported by Brunt" to have pronounced the Anabaptist's sentence in the few words scarcely less impious than unfeeling: *"Qui iterum mergit, mergatur."*

Not to Calvin does the world owe the idea or the practice of *religious liberty*, or even *toleration;* for "he instigated the persecuting laws of Geneva, and he it was who had arrested, condemned, and roasted, in *a slow fire of green wood*, the martyr SERVETUS."

Mosheim, a Lutheran himself, confesses "there were certain sects and doctors, against whom the zeal, vigilance, and severity of Catholics, Lutherans, and Calvinists were united. *The objects of their common aversion were the Anabaptists.*" And it has been so from that day to the present.

The sentiments of the Baptists, which were then so disliked by statesmen, clergy, Protestants and Papists, and for which Baptists are to-day everywhere persecuted and oppressed by

Protestants and Papists, are thus stated by Orchard:

"We have recorded that the Baptists were the common objects of aversion to Catholics, Lutherans, and Calvinists, whose united zeal was directed to their destruction. So deeply were these prejudices interwoven with the State party, that the knights on oath were to declare their abhorrence of Anabaptism. The sentiments of these people, and which were so disliked by statesmen, clergy, and reformers, may be stated under five views, viz.: " A love of civil liberty in opposition to magisterial dominion; an affirmation of the sufficiency and simplicity of revelation, in opposition to scholastic theology; a zeal for self-government, in opposition to clerical authority; a requisition of the reasonable service of a personal profession of Christianity rising out of man's own convictions, in opposition to the practice of force on infants—the whole of which they deem superstition or enthusiasm; and the indispensable necessity of virtue in every individual member of a Christian Church, in distinction from all speculative creeds, all rites and ceremonies, and parochial divisions.' These views, to the statesman, were adverse to his line of policy with his peasants; to the clergy they were offensive, since it placed every man on a level with the priesthood, and sanctioned one to instruct another; to the Reformers they were objectionable, since they broke the national tie, and allowed all persons equal liberty to think, choose, and act in the affairs of the soul: thus these sentiments were the aversion of all. An edict issued by Frederick, at a later period, shows how unpalatable these views were. His majesty expressed his astonishment at the number of Anabaptists, and his horror at the principal error which they embraced, which was, that, according to the express declaration of the Holy Scriptures, (1 Cor. vii: 23,) they were to submit to no human authority. He adds that his conscience compelled him to proscribe them, and accordingly he banished them from his dominions on pain of death."

We claim that Baptists were the first assertors of the principle of religious liberty in England. Mr. Williams, in speaking of the times of Cromwell, and the events of that period, says:

"The share which the Baptists took in shoring up the fallen liberties of England, and in infusing new vigor and liberality into the constitution of that country, is not generally known. Yet to this body, English liberty owes a debt it can never acknowledge. Among the Baptists, Christian freedom found its earliest, its stanchest, its most consistent, and its most disinterested champions."

We maintain, what authentic and received history so abundantly affirms, that Baptists were the first assertors of religious liberty in New England or on the American Continent. The first blood shed on these shores for religious liberty was Baptist blood, and it followed the excoriating lash, driven by Pedobaptist hands, by the order of a Pedobaptist court, under the direction of a Protestant State Church in New England. The last persons imprisoned in America for preaching the Gospel were Baptists. We maintain that Baptists, singly and alone, and in face of the bitter opposition of Episcopalians, Presbyterians, and Methodists, severed the Church and State in Virginia, and abolished all laws oppressive to the conscience, and thus secured in the Old Dominion the triumph of civil and religious liberty. We maintain that America is indebted solely to Baptists, first, for the *idea* of a pure Democratic form of civil government, and then for having prepared the popular mind by the molding influence of their principles to receive such a government, as well as for its present strength and sole hope of its perpetuity.

The following facts were communicated to the *Christian Watchman*, several years ago, by the Rev. Dr. Fishback, of Lexington, Ky.:

"Mr. Editor: The following circumstance, which occurred in the State of Virginia, relative to Mr. Jefferson, was detailed to me by Elder Andrew Tribble, about six years ago, who since died when ninety-two or three years old. The facts may interest some of your readers.

"Andrew Tribble was the pastor of a small Baptist Church which held monthly meetings at a short distance from Mr. Jefferson's house, eight or ten years before the American Revolution. Mr. Jefferson attended the meetings of the Church several months in succession, and after one of them he asked Elder Tribble to go home and dine with him, with which he complied.

"Mr. Tribble asked Mr. Jefferson how he was pleased with their Church government? Mr. Jefferson replied that it had struck him with great force, and had interested him much; that he considered it the only form of *pure democracy* that then existed in the world, and had concluded that it would be the *best plan of government for the American colonies.* This was several years before the Declaration of Independence."

Gervinus, the most astute and philosophic historian of his age, in his work entitled, "An Introduction to the History of the Nineteenth Century," says:

"In accordance with these principles, Roger Williams insisted in Massachusetts upon allowing entire freedom of conscience, and upon entire separation of the Church and the State. But he was obliged to flee, and in 1636 he formed in Rhode Island a small and new society, in which perfect freedom in matters of faith was allowed, and in which the majority ruled in all civil affairs. Here, in a little State, the fundamental principles of political and ecclesiastical liberty practically prevailed, before they were even taught in any of the schools of philosophy in Europe. At that time people predicted only a short existence for these democratical experiments—universal suffrage, universal eligibility to office, the annual change of rulers, perfect religious freedom—the Miltonian doctrines of schisms. But not only have these ideas and these forms of government maintained themselves here, but precisely from this little State have they extended themselves throughout the United States. They have conquered the aristocratic tendencies in Carolina and New York, the High Church in Virginia, the theocracy in Massachusetts, and the monarchy in all America. They have given laws to a continent, and, formidable through their moral influence, *they lie at the bottom of all the democratic movements which are now shaking the nations of Europe.*"

In his historical "Memoirs of the English Catholics," Charles Butler makes allusion, as follows, to our Baptist fathers:

"It is observable that this denomination of Christians, now truly respectable, but in their origin as little intellectual as any, first propagated the principles of religious liberty."

We take a sincere pride in the fact that Baptists were the earliest witnesses for soul-freedom. Others have but followed in their track. They led the way, and made it clear to the vision of trampled nations, by pouring out their own blood to make it. This noble blow, struck before all others, in the warfare against spiritual despotism, should live for them, in the mind of the world, an enduring monument of hopeful and emulative remembrance. Yet, for our principles, we have been everywhere spoken against. Says Underhill :

"The Papists abhorred the Baptists; for, if their doctrines prevailed, a Church hoary with age, laden with the spoils of many lands, rich in the merchandise of souls, must be broken down and destroyed. The Protestants hated them; for their cherished headship, their worldly alliances, the pomps and circumstances of State religion, must be debased before the kingly crown of Jesus. The Puritans defamed them; for Baptist sentiments were too liberal and free for those who sought a Papal authority over conscience, and desired the sword of the higher powers to enforce their wily discipline."

Says Shelden & Willard :

" The Baptists have ever been the firm friends and supporters of religious liberty. The right which they claim for themselves of professing their own religion, they cheerfully concede to all. To punish men for religious opinions peaceably asserted, without injury to civil society, they consider as persecution."

Papists and Protestants have united in the destruction of Baptists.

"During the wars of the Reformation, the Papists and Protestants destroyed each other in every possible manner. Never were enemies more bitter or uncompromising. In but one thing only was it possible for them to agree, and that was the persecution of Baptists. Here they harmonized perfectly; and it is remarkable that in several of their treaties, as recorded by Dr. Merle D'Aubigné, special articles were inserted, binding both parties to use every possible effort to destroy all the Baptists in Europe."—*Address before the American Baptist Historical Society.*

Baptists are still prosecuting their great mission in England and Europe, remonstrating against the iniquitous union of Church and State, and pleading with Protestants to grant universal liberty of conscience in religion.

The British *Banner*, of July 10, 1850, states that a petition was presented from one hundred and twenty ministers and delegates of the Associated Baptist Churches of Yorkshire, praying for the separation of Church and State, and that the national property, hitherto engrossed by a few sects, might be devoted to secular and really useful purposes.

Let monarchists and Papists hate and sneer at Baptists, but, with these facts before their eyes, how can true-hearted American republicans and patriots? With such a history, honored and pre-eminently illustrious as is the very name of Baptist by the glories of such principles and such heroic achievements under such sacrifices, Baptists can afford to bear the odium attempted to be cast upon them by the descendants of those who shed their blood.

"Many attempts have been made to exterminate them. Like their earlier brethren, 'they had trial of cruel mockings and scourgings, yea, moreover, of bonds and imprisonment; they were stoned, they were sawn asunder, were tempted, were slain with the sword; they wandered about in sheep-skins and goat-skins, being destitute, afflicted, tormented. * * * They wandered in deserts, and in mountains, and in dens and caves of the earth.' But the 'blood of the martyrs was the seed of the Church.' Light has succeeded darkness, hope despair, prosperity has followed adversity, and to-day the Baptist denomination stands as a monument to the faithfulness of God, in fulfilling his promises to those who love, follow, and trust him."

I can say, in closing this brief review of our principles and history, with a brother "Anabaptist:"

"We feel no blush of shame mantling our cheeks as we trace the history of our fathers. True they were not great according to the world's estimate of greatness. They were not noble after any human standard patent of nobility. Our Church did not spring into existence at the mandate of royalty. Our doctrines were not warmed into life by the sunshine of court favor. Our people did not occupy the high places of worldly dignity. They were the outcasts of the outcast. They were the persecuted of the persecuted. They were counted unworthy to dwell with those who were themselves the victims of proscription. But they were among the moral heroes whose characters brighten under the searching light of history; and they have left to their descendants a name which they may be proud to bear, and an example which they should be zealous to emulate.

"They have swelled that list of confessors and martyrs to whom the world is slow to render its acknowledgment. But their record is on high, and their time is sure."

"Their blood was shed
In confirmation of the noblest claim,—
Our claim to feed upon immortal truth,
To walk with God, to be divinely free,
To soar and to anticipate the skies.
Yet few remember them. They lived unknown,
Till persecution dragged them into fame,
And chased them up to heaven. Their ashes flew—
No marble tells us whither. With their names
No bard embalms and sanctifies his song,
And history, so warm on meaner themes,
Is cold on this."

APPENDIX.

SINCE writing the above, the following additional facts have come to our knowledge:

This question was recently up before the Free Church Presbytery of Kingston, Canada, and after discussing the question they came to the conclusion "that it ought not to be considered Christian baptism, and that when converts from Romanism are admitted into the Church, they ought to receive the rite anew."

The validity of Romish baptisms was likewise discussed in the Presbytery of Montreal, and it was decided that such baptisms were invalid. But the vote was a "tie vote," and this result was only secured by the casting vote of the Moderator!

We take the following facts from the public journals:

"The Portuguese Protestants who came to this country several years ago, and settled at Springfield and Jacksonville, Illinois, are still in trouble—the Old School Presbyterians requiring that they shall be baptized by a Presbyterian clergyman, and they, or a large portion of them, including Rev. Alphonso Demattos, insisting that the baptism received by them in the Roman Catholic Church, before leaving Madeira, is sufficient. The matter is now before the committee appointed by the Presbytery."

Will the Old School Presbyterians receive their baptism in the face of the decision of the General Assembly, given in 1845?

But the most recent case is that of the celebrated Father Chiniquay, of Kankakee, Illinois, who recently protested against, and came out of the Catholic Church, with about two thousand of his flock. Within the present month,* he, with most of his people, have been received by the Kankakee Presbytery, (Old School Presbyte-

---

* January, 1860.

rians,) *with their Romish baptisms*, and this Father Chiniquay has been appointed to a charge by the Presbytery, without either *baptism* or *ordination!*

What will be the final result of this act on the part of this Presbytery? Will not other Presbyteries take an appeal to the next General Assembly? And if the question is again taken, then will the Assembly "back down," and reverse its former decision, or will it reaffirm it with a formidable schism threatening it?

It strikes me that the next Old School Assembly will find itself in a dilemma.

A HISTORICAL FACT.

POPE STEPHEN THE AUTHOR OF SPRINKLING.

The Rt. Rev. J. T. M. Trevern, D. D., Bishop of Strasburg, a high dignitary of the Catholic Church, in 1847, wrote a book in defense of his Church, called "The Discussion Amicale." It was addressed in the form of letters to the clergy of every Protestant communion, but especially to those of the Church of England.

The object of the work was to show the inconsistencies of Protestants in proclaiming the word of God as their only rule, while they follow the traditions of Rome. On page 147, vol. ii, he says:

"The clergy of Elizabeth, in unison with the innovators of the continent, and, like them, in opposition to the sacred books and antiquity, declared accordingly, that the holy Scripture containeth all things necessary to salvation; so that whatsoever is not read therein, or can not be proved thereby, is not to be required of any man that it should be believed as an article of faith, or be thought requisite or necessary to salvation. But, without going any further, show us, my lords, the validity of your baptism, by Scripture alone! Jesus Christ there ordains that it shall be conferred, not by pouring water on the heads of believers, but by believers plunging into water.

"The word *baptizo*, employed by the Evangelists, strictly conveys this signification, *as the learned are agreed*, and at the head of them Casaubon, of all Calvinists the best learned in the Greek language. Now baptism by immersion has ceased for many ages, (among those whom this man esteem Christians, we, Anabaptists, who always used immersion, he did not esteem Christians,) and you yourselves, as well as we, have only received it by infusion. It would, therefore, be all up with your baptism unless you established it by tradition and the practice of the Church, (*i. e.*, Roman Catholic.) This being settled, I ask you from whom have you received baptism? Is it **not** from the Church of Rome? And what do you think of her? Do you not consider her as heretical, and even idolatrous? You can not then, according to the terms of Scripture, prove the validity of your baptism, and to produce a plea for it, you are obliged to seek it with Pope Stephen, and the Councils of Arles and Nice, in Apostolic tradition."

This is the testimony of one of the most distinguished scholars in the Catholic Church, bearing testimony to a historical fact. Can his testimony be set aside?

A BIOGRAPHICAL SKETCH OF JAMES ROBINSON GRAVES (1820-1893)

BY

JOHN FRANKLIN JONES

A Biographical Sketch of James Robinson Graves (1820-1893)

James Robinson Graves was born in Chester, Vermont April 10, 1820. Left fatherless at two weeks, his widowed mother defrauded of her husband's estate by the husband's business partner, the young Graves moved with his mother and sister to northern Ohio at nineteen. Of Congregation heritage, he had joined a Baptist church at age fifteen (*ESB*).

He became principal of a school, despite his being without significant schooling himself. Graves learned the night before the subject matter he taught each day. He took charge of the school at Nicholasville, Kentucky in 1841. He taught himself a language each of the next four years and completed a college-degree equivalent. He studied the Bible in detail and joined Mount Freedom Baptist Church. That church licensed him to preach and ordained him in 1844 (*ESB*).

John moved to Nashville, Tennessee in July 1845 to teach, and he joined the First Baptist Church of that city. He became the pastor of Second Baptist (later, Central) and served that church for approximately one year (*ESB*).

Graves became assistant editor of *The Baptist* upon its being given to the Baptist General Association of Tennessee and North Alabama in 1846 by Robet Boyté Crawford Howell. Along with A. B. Shankland, he was made publisher and depository agent for the paper and established a bookstore (*ESB*).

Graves succeeded Howell as editor in June 1848 and edited the paper through its tenure as *The Baptist* and the *Tennessee Baptist* until August, 1889, when it became the *Baptist and Reflector*. For a number of years after 1869, it was the official paper for the Baptists of Arkansas, Louisiana, Mississippi, and Tennessee (*ESB*).

Graves led the Landmark movement from its beginning in 1853, working fervently to make it the dominant perspective among Southern Baptists. He led a pointed, but unsuccessful, effort to remove from the Foreign Mission Board the power "to examine, choose, support, and direct missionaries." He was convinced that those actions belonged exclusively to churches, associations, or groups of churches. Though they debated Graves' proposal for several hours at Richmond, Virginia, in May 1859, the messengers of the Convention voted to continue the its current practice related to missionaries (*ESB*).

Strongly committed to the importance of Sunday schools and Sunday school libraries, Graves became "a severe and sustained critic" of the "theological deviations" and insensitivity to existing needs by the SBC's publishing arm, the Southern Baptist Publication Society, Charleston, South Carolina. He led the effort to establish a thoroughly Landmark competitor in the Southern Baptist Sunday School Union (1857) and two associated publishing houses. One effort collapsed in 1871 and the other in 1877 (*ESB*).

He organized three tract societies (1847, 1869, 1883) and the Nashville Indian and Missionary Association (1846), enabling him to maintain his continuing interest in the Indians. He was one of several leaders who started Mary Sharpe College for women at Winchester, Tennessee (1850) and raised funds to endow a theology chair at Union University. He also founded, edited, and published (for six years) the quarterly, *The Christian Review* (1855-60) (*ESB*).

A Biographical Sketch of James Robinson Graves

Graves authored *The Desire of All Nations, The Watchman's Reply, The Trilemma, The First Baptist Church in America, The Great Iron Wheel, The Little Iron Wheel, The Bible Doctrine of the Middle Life, Expositions of Modern Spiritism, The Little Seraph, Old Landmarkism, What Is It?*, and *The Work of Christ in Seven Dispensations*. With James Madison Pendleton, he published *The Southern Psalmist* (1858) and compiled/published *The New Baptist Psalmist for Churches and Sunday Schools* (1873) (*ESB*).

J. R. Graves "influenced Southern Baptist life of the 19th century in more ways, and probably to a greater degree, than any other person." An agitator and a controversialist, he kept Southern Baptists in "almost continual and often bitter controversy for about 30 years." He frequently and prolongedly debated persons of other denominations. Though magnetic and dynamic, he was "acrimonious in his disputations and attacks." He often held large crowds raptly attentive for hours during his lengthy orations (*ESB*).

Graves suffered a paralyzing stroke August 17, 1884 while preaching at First Baptist Church, Memphis. He experienced a side-crushing fall in his yard in early 1889, which fall left him confined to a wheelchair for the remainder of his life. Though he continued to publish *The Baptist*, he gave less attention to controversial matters. He died June 26, 1893 in Memphis, Tennessee (*ESB*).

BIBLIOGRAPHY

Cathcart, William, ed. *The Baptist Encyclopaedia: A Dictionary of the Doctrines, Ordinances, Usages, Confessions of Faith, Sufferings, Labors, and Successes, and of the General History of the Baptist Denomination in All Lands, with Numerous Biographical Sketches of Distinguished American and Foreign Baptist, and a Supplement*. Philadelphia, Louis H. Everts, 1881; reprint, Paris, AR: Baptist Standard Bearer, 1988. S.v. "Graves, J. R., LL.D."

JOHN FRANKLIN JONES

Encyclopedia of Southern Baptists,. S.v. "Graves, James Robinson," by Homer L. Grice.

BY JOHN FRANKLIN JONES
CORDOVA, TENNESSEE
JUNE 2006

THE BAPTIST STANDARD BEARER, INC.

a non-profit, tax-exempt corporation
committed to the Publication & Preservation
of the Baptist Heritage.

CURRENT TITLES AVAILABLE IN
THE BAPTIST *DISTINCTIVES* SERIES

KIFFIN, WILLIAM A Sober Discourse of Right to Church-Communion. Wherein is proved by Scripture, the Example of the Primitive Times, and the Practice of All that have Professed the Christian Religion: That no Unbaptized person may be Regularly admitted to the Lord's Supper. (London: George Larkin, 1681).

KINGHORN, JOSEPH Baptism, A Term of Communion. (Norwich: Bacon, Kinnebrook, and Co., 1816)

KINGHORN, JOSEPH A Defense of "Baptism, A Term of Communion". In Answer To Robert Hall's Reply. (Norwich: Wilkin and Youngman, 1820).

GILL, JOHN Gospel Baptism. A Collection of Sermons, Tracts, etc., on Scriptural Authority, the Nature of the New Testament Church and the Ordinance of Baptism by John Gill. (Paris, AR: The Baptist Standard Bearer, Inc., 2006).

CARSON, ALEXANDER	Ecclesiastical Polity of the New Testament. (Dublin: William Carson, 1856).
BOOTH, ABRAHAM	A Defense of the Baptists. A Declaration and Vindication of Three Historically Distinctive Baptist Principles. Compiled and Set Forth in the Republication of Three Books. Revised edition. (Paris, AR: The Baptist Standard Bearer, Inc., 2006).
BOOTH, ABRAHAM	Paedobaptism Examined on the Principles, Concessions, and Reasonings of the Most Learned Paedobaptists. With Replies to the Arguments and Objections of Dr. Williams and Mr. Peter Edwards. 3 volumes. (London: Ebenezer Palmer, 1829).
CARROLL, B. H.	*Ecclesia* - The Church. With an Appendix. (Louisville: Baptist Book Concern, 1903).
CHRISTIAN, JOHN T.	Immersion, The Act of Christian Baptism. (Louisville: Baptist Book Concern, 1891).
FROST, J. M.	Pedobaptism: Is It From Heaven Or Of Men? (Philadelphia: American Baptist Publication Society, 1875).
FULLER, RICHARD	Baptism, and the Terms of Communion; An Argument. (Charleston, SC: Southern Baptist Publication Society, 1854).
GRAVES, J. R.	Tri-Lemma: or, Death By Three Horns. The Presbyterian General Assembly Not Able To Decide This Question: "Is Baptism In The Romish Church Valid?" 1st Edition.

	(Nashville: Southwestern Publishing House, 1861).
MELL, P.H.	Baptism In Its Mode and Subjects. (Charleston, SC: Southern Baptist Publications Society, 1853).
JETER, JEREMIAH B.	Baptist Principles Reset. Consisting of Articles on Distinctive Baptist Principles by Various Authors. With an Appendix. (Richmond: The Religious Herald Co., 1902).
PENDLETON, J.M.	Distinctive Principles of Baptists. (Philadelphia: American Baptist Publication Society, 1882).
THOMAS, JESSE B.	The Church and the Kingdom. A New Testament Study. (Louisville: Baptist Book Concern, 1914).
WALLER, JOHN L.	Open Communion Shown to be Unscriptural & Deleterious. With an introductory essay by Dr. D. R. Campbell and an Appendix. (Louisville: Baptist Book Concern, 1859).

For a complete list of current authors/titles, visit our internet site at:
www.standardbearer.org
or write us at:

he Baptist Standard Bearer, Inc.

NUMBER ONE IRON OAKS DRIVE • PARIS, ARKANSAS 72855
TEL # 479-963-3831   FAX # 479-963-8083
EMAIL: Baptist@centurytel.net   http://www.standardbearer.org

Thou hast given a standard to them that fear thee; that it may be displayed because of the truth. — Psalm 60:4

www.ingramcontent.com/pod-product-compliance
Lightning Source LLC
Chambersburg PA
CBHW020804160426
43192CB00006B/429